Athens

DIRECTIONS

WRITTEN AND RESEARCHED BY

John Fisher and

Paul Hellander

NEW YORK • LONDON • DELHI

www.roughguides.com

Contents

Introduction to Athens

In most minds, Athens is a city that happened two-and-a-half thousand years ago, and it's true that even now that past looms large – literally, in the shape of the mighty Acropolis that dominates almost every view, as well as in every visitor's itinerary. Yet Athens is also home to over four million people, more than a third of the Greek population and is very much a city for the twenty-first century, one that has transformed itself for the 2004 Olympics.

For many, the stunning remains of the ancient Classical Greek city are the highlight of any visit. The National Archeological Museum has the finest collection of Greek antiquities in the world, and there are plenty of smaller specialist museums. Even on a brief visit, however, it is a shame to see Athens purely as the repository of ancient sites and museum pieces. It's worth taking the time to explore some of the city's

When to visit

Athens is at its most agreeable outside the peak period of **early July** to the end of **August**, when soaring temperatures (sometimes over 40°C), plus crowds of foreigners and locals alike, can be overpowering. Perhaps the best months to visit are **May to early June**, **September** and **October** – temperatures are pleasant (20°C and upwards), and visitors fewer. In **April** you can also see lovely displays of spring flowers on the surrounding mountains. The **winter** months can be very cold, and February is often rainy.

▲ Byzantine Mosaic

neighbourhoods: in particular, the old nineteenth-century quarter of Pláka has a delightful mix of Turkish, Neoclassical and Greek island-style architecture and intriguing little museums devoted to traditional arts, from ceramics to musical instruments. Here you'll also encounter scattered relics of the Byzantine and medieval town that captivated Byron and the Romantics. Just to the north of Pláka, the bazaar area around Athinás and Eólou retains an almost Middle Eastern atmosphere, while the National Gardens and elegant Kolonáki offer respite from the bustling city. Still well within the limits of Greater Athens are the peaceful monasteries of Kessarianí and Dhafní, the latter with Byzantine mosaics the equal of any in Greece.

There are spectacular bird's-eye views from the central hills of Lykavitós and Filopáppou, while more adventurous walkers can head for the mountains that ring the city. Springtime hikes here reveal the astonishing range of Greek wild flowers – especially on the vast, largely unspoilt slopes of Mount Párnitha.

Outside the city itself you'll find more ancient sites, while sun-worshippers flock to the suburban beach resorts. There's the chance to escape to the islands, too, several of which can be reached from the busy port of Pireás in just a couple of hours.

For some, however, the biggest surprise in Athens is the vibrant life of the city itself. Cafés are packed day and night, and the streets stay lively until 3 or 4am, with some of the best bars and clubs in the country. Eating out is great, with establishments ranging from lively tavernas to the finest gourmet restaurants. In summer much of the action takes place outdoors, complemented by open-air films, concerts and classical drama. The extraordinarily diverse shopping scene ranges from colourful bazaars and lively street markets to chic shopping malls filled with the latest designer goods. And with a good-value public transport system – particularly the newly expanded metro – you'll have no difficulty getting around.

◂ Neoclassical statue

◂ Kolonáki

>> ATHENS AT A GLANCE

National Archeological museum

The Acropolis

The Acropolis remains the city's biggest attraction. Dominating its southern slope is the restored second-century Roman Herodes Atticus Theatre, a spectacular setting for performances of music and Classical drama during the summer festival.

Pláka Street

The National Archeological Museum

By far the most important museum in Athens, the National Archeological Museum houses the world's greatest collection of Cycladic, Minoan, Mycenaean and Classical Greek art.

Kolonáki

For fashionable shopping, Kolonáki is the city's most chic central district. Should you tire of hunting for the latest designer gear, you'll find some great pavement cafés and restaurants – or come here at night for the bars and buzzing live music venues.

Pláka

The largely pedestrianized area of Pláka, with its narrow lanes and stepped alleys climbing towards the Acropolis, is perhaps the most attractive part of Athens. It's

Herodes Atticus Theatre

◂ Delphi

touristy, but full of atmosphere and the city's best for idle wandering.

Cape Soúnio

Cape Soúnio's dramatic setting overlooking the Aegean has made it a landmark for centuries to boats sailing between Pireás and the islands. Its tremendous views and evocative Temple of Poseidon certainly impressed Byron – who carved his name on one of the pillars.

Monastiráki

While less touristy than Pláka, Monastiráki still has great opportunities for eating, drinking and above all shopping – from flea markets to upmarket designer shops. Often busy and noisy, you'll still find the occasional quiet oasis in the high-rise urban surroundings.

Delphi

Set amongst the massive crags of Mount Parnassós, Delphi is the site of the most important oracle in ancient Greece. Today, its awe-inspiring ruins and spectacular setting make it one of the most memorable excursions from Athens.

◂ Monastiráki

Ideas

The big six

Athens is still defined above all by the brief period of glory it enjoyed in the fifth century BC – the Golden Age of **Classical Athens**. The signature image of the city, and an absolute must-see, is the rocky hill of the **Acropolis**, topped by the Parthenon. Smaller, lesser-known ancient sites are scattered throughout the city centre. The city's Archeological Museum, too, is one of the world's greatest, with treasures not just from Athens but from all the cultures of ancient Greece. The modern city is not always beautiful, but it is enjoyable, with its buzzing outdoor restaurants and cafés, great nightlife, and easy access to a spectacular coastline.

National Archeological Museum

The gold Mask of Agamemnon from Mycenae is the biggest crowd-puller in Athens' premier museum.

P.96 THE NATIONAL ARCHEOLOGICAL MUSEUM, EXÁRHIA & NEÁPOLI

Lykavitós Hill

Climb Lykavitós Hill – or take the funicular – for spectacular views of the city, including the Acropolis.

P.104 KOLONÁKI AND LYKAVITÓS HILL

Acropolis

Crowned by the Parthenon, and surrounded by the major relics of ancient Athens, the Acropolis is one of the archetypal images of Western civilization.

▸ P.51 ▸ THE ACROPOLIS ▲

Tower of the Winds

On the site of the Roman Forum, the intriguing and well-preserved Tower of the Winds is compass, weather vane, sundial and water-clock in one.

▸ P.71 ▸ MONASTIRÁKI & PSYRRÍ ▼

Street life

In summer, life in Athens moves on to the streets, terraces and roof gardens. Dining or drinking al fresco, with the Acropolis as backdrop, can be an unforgettable experience.

▸ P.85 ▸ THISSÍO, GÁZI & ÁNO PETRÁLONA ▲

Temple of Poseidon

Dominating Cape Sounío, the Temple of Poseidon commands magnificent views of the seas and islands around Athens.

▸ P.133 ▸ ATTICA ▼

Acropolis

Exploring the Acropolis and its surrounds can easily absorb an entire day. While the **Parthenon** is the most imposing of the remains atop the steep-sided hill, it's far from the only one; the Acropolis has an extraordinary concentration of superlative Classical architecture, all of it dating from just a few decades at the height of ancient Athenian democracy. The **Acropolis Museum** houses many of the treasures from the site and hopes one day to complete its collection with the returned Parthenon Marbles.

The Erectheion

The most sacred of the ancient temples and a superb example of Ionic architecture, the Erectheion's south porch is supported by six larger-than-life maidens – the Caryatids.

▸P.56 ▸ THE ACROPOLIS ▲

The Parthenon Marbles

Part of the pediment of the Parthenon has been reconstructed in the Acropolis Museum – although the Elgin Marbles remain in the British Museum, despite a long Greek campaign to reclaim them.

▸P.56 ▸ THE ACROPOLIS ▼

The Propylaia

The imposing entrance to the Acropolis now as in Classical times, the Propylaia were considered by ancient Athenians to be their most prestigious monument.

▶ P.53 ▶ THE ACROPOLIS ▲

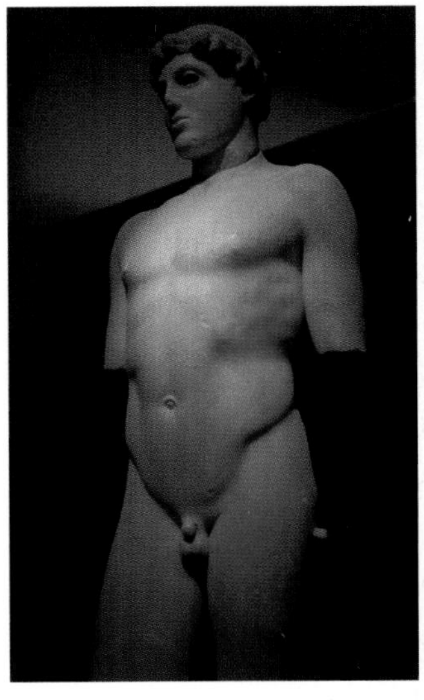

Acropolis Museum

Containing almost all the treasures removed from the site since the 1830s, the museum includes fine sculptures that once adorned the Acropolis buildings, such as the *Kritias Boy* pictured here.

▶ P.57 ▶ THE ACROPOLIS ▶

Acropolis son et lumière

The Acropolis is spectacularly lit at night throughout the summer, effects that can be enjoyed from vantage points across the city.

▶ P.51 ▶ THE ACROPOLIS ▼

Classical Athens

In the fifth century BC, the city-state of Athens suddenly found itself secure and wealthy, having defeated the Persians and risen to dominate their mainland rivals. They celebrated their success by a radical experiment with **democracy**, and with a flourishing of **art**, **architecture**, **literature** and **philosophy** whose influences imbue Western culture to this day. The physical remains of the Classical Golden Age are still to be seen everywhere in Athens, and with the city's reconstruction more is emerging almost daily.

Kerameikos

A tranquil, little-visited site that incorporates the cemetery of ancient Athens as well as fragments of the city walls, gates and the roads that led to them.

▸ P.83 ▸ THISSÍO, GÁZI & ÁNO PETRÁLONA

Temple of Athena Nike

Small but perfectly formed, this temple to Athens' patron goddess encapsulates the ideals of Classical architecture.

▸P.55 ▸ THE ACROPOLIS ▲

Stoa of Attalos

The reconstruction of the Stoa of Attalos, part of the ancient Athenian marketplace, shows how Classical Athens might have looked in its heyday, and houses the Museum of the Agora.

▸P.60 ▸ THE ACROPOLIS ▼

Theatre of Dionysos

The stunning theatre where the masterpieces of Classical drama were first performed.

▸P.57 ▸ THE ACROPOLIS ▲

Monument of Lysikratos

In a quiet corner of Pláka, this is a lone survivor of what was once a long line of similar monuments celebrating victory in ancient drama contests.

▸P.64 ▸ PLÁKA ▼

Roman Athens

The **Romans** controlled Athens for some eight hundred years, but they left relatively few monuments. On the whole they respected the artistic and architectural heritage of Classical Athens, while the city itself became something of a backwater of the Empire. There were, however, two great benefactors in particular whose legacy has survived: the **Emperor Hadrian** and **Herodes Atticus**, a wealthy Roman senator.

Hadrian's Library

You can only admire it from the other side of a fence, but the scale of the Emperor's structure is truly impressive.

▸ P.74 ▸ MONASTIRÁKI & PSYRRÍ ▲

Tower of the Winds

Situated in the Roman forum, this curious yet graceful octagonal tower has each of its well-preserved faces decorated with a relief of the eight winds.

▸ P.71 ▸ MONASTIRÁKI & PSYRRÍ ▲

The Roman Forum

Built by Julius and Augustus Caesar as an extension of the busy Greek marketplace, the Roman Forum is one of the main attractions in Monastiráki. The site includes the oldest Mosque in Athens, the Fethiye Tzami.

▸P.70 ▸ MONASTIRÁKI & PSYRRÍ ▲

Hadrian's Arch

Erected by Hadrian to mark the division between the ancient Greek city and the modern Roman one, this imposing arch rises to a height of eighteen metres.

▸P.115 ▸ SÝNDAGMA & AROUND ▼

The Areopagus

This low, rocky hill below the Acropolis has rich historical significance: in ancient times it was the site of the Council of Nobles and the Judicial Court, and later St Paul preached here, setting in train the conversion of Athens to Christianity.

▸P.59 ▸ THE ACROPOLIS ▲

Odeion of Herodes Atticus

The partly reconstructed theatre at the foot of the Acropolis is today a stunning setting for events at the annual Hellenic festival.

▸P.58 ▸ THE ACROPOLIS ▲

Byzantine Athens

When the Roman empire split, Athens came under the control of **Byzantium** (Constantinople) and the Byzantine empire. The schools of philosophy were closed, and many of the city's "pagan" temples converted to **churches**. The legacy of the early Christians is a series of beautiful ancient monasteries, as well as museums and wonderful frescoes and icons.

Kapnikaréa

The eleventh-century church of Kapnikaréa, right in the heart of Athens, makes for an extraordinary contrast to the packed shopping streets surrounding it.

P.75 ▸ MONASTIRÁKI & PSYRRÍ

Byzantine and Christian Museum

The richness of many of the icons on display is typical of the Byzantine era's artistic styles.

▸ P.106 ▸ KOLONÁKI AND LYKAVITÓS ▸

Christ Pantokrator

Christ sits in majesty at the heart of the world-famous cycle of mosaics in Dhafní Monastery.

▸ P.125 ▸ SUBURBAN ATHENS ▾

Dhafní Monastery

The fortress-like exterior of the Monastery of Dhafní, on the western fringes of Athens, gives little clue of the glories within.

▸ P.123 ▸ SUBURBAN ATHENS ▾

Archeological Museum

Athens' National Archeological Museum is among the world's greatest museums, with an unrivalled collection of **ancient Greek art**. It spans every era from prehistoric and the development of **Mycenaean** and **Minoan** culture, through **Classical Greece** and on to **Roman** and early **Byzantine** times. Extensive renovation for the 2004 Olympics has provided a setting to match the contents. Highlights are the finds from graves at Mycenae, and from the excavations of Akrotíri on the island of Thíra (Santorini).

The museum building

The imposing Neoclassical building housing the Museum occupies an entire block, set back from the street amid jungly gardens.

▸P.96 ▸ THE ARCHEOLOGICAL MUSEUM, EXÁRHIA & NEÁPOLI ▲

The Vafio Cup

This wonderful gold cup, one of two dating from around 1500 BC, depicts a bull being trapped, and was made by beating the gold into a hollow mould.

▸P.96 ▸ THE ARCHEOLOGICAL MUSEUM, EXÁRHIA & NEÁPOLI ▲

Poseidon

In this graceful bronze statue from the mid-fifth century BC, Poseidon stands poised in perfect balance as he prepares to hurl his (missing) trident.

▸P.98 ▸ THE ARCHEOLOGICAL MUSEUM, EXÁRHIA & NEÁPOLI ▼

Frescoes

The Archeological Museum holds an important collection of frescoes; this example from Akrotíri depicts two boys boxing, its style clearly influenced by Minoan Crete.

▸P.96 ▸ THE ARCHEOLOGICAL MUSEUM, EXÁRHIA & NEÁPOLI ▲

The Little Jockey of Artemission

In another masterpiece of animated bronze sculpture, the delicate-looking rider – probably a boy – seems far too small for his galloping mount.

▸P.98 ▸ THE ARCHEOLOGICAL MUSEUM, EXÁRHIA & NEÁPOLI ▼

Cultural museums

The city's lesser-known museums should not be overlooked. Among the best are the **Benáki** and **Kanellópoulos museums**, each housing magnificent private collections that cover every age of Greek art and history from the prehistoric era to the nineteenth-century independence struggle. Others are more specialist: for example, the **Goulandhrís Museum of Cycladic Art** concentrates on artefacts predating the Classical era, superbly displayed, while the **Museum of Greek Folk Art** features ceramics, jewellery, weaving and other crafts.

Kanellopoulou Museum

Right under the Acropolis at the top of Pláka, the Kanellopoulou Museum fills a former private home with a treasure trove of fine art.

▸ P.65 ▸ PLÁKA ▲

Museum of Greek Popular Musical Instruments

Superbly displayed in a Neoclassical building, the museum traces the history of virtually every type of instrument ever played in Greece.

▸ P.73 ▸ MONASTIRÁKI & PSYRRÍ ▲

Museum of Greek Folk Art

A superb collection of arts and crafts, including regional costumes and shadow puppets.

▸P.61 ▸ PLÁKA ▲

Benáki Museum

Occupying a graceful nineteenth-century mansion, the Benáki collection is of exceptional variety and quality.

▸P.105 ▸ KOLONÁKI & LYKAVITÓS HILL ▼

Goulandhrís Museum of Cycladic and Ancient Greek Art

This small collection is extremely well presented, and contains fine examples of Cycladic art.

▸P.105 ▸ KOLONÁKI & LYKAVITÓS HILL ▲

Modern Athens

Plans for a city of broad boulevards, drawn up in the nineteenth century when Athens became capital after Independence, didn't survive long. After World War II, instead, rapid growth saw the city emerge as a vibrant, stimulating and exciting mix of East and West, urban and rural, where chickens roost next to Internet cafés, and eastern-style bazaars vie for space with chic outlets of Armani and Zara.

The metro

The development of new metro lines has helped transform the city centre, cutting traffic and pollution and providing fast, efficient and easy-to-use transport.

▸ P.166 ▸ ESSENTIALS

Platía Omonías

A great central meeting point; its perimeter is lined with kiosks selling everything from papers and lottery tickets to watch-straps.

▶P.88 ▶ PLATÍA OMONÍAS & AROUND 

The Voulí

The vast Neoclassical Greek parliament building is guarded by *evzones*, goose-stepping in colourful traditional costume.

▶P.114 ▶ SÝNDAGMA & AROUND 

Platía Sýndagmatos

Sýndagma Square is the vital heart of the modern city, bounded on one side by the parliament building and surrounded by bustling commercial streets.

▶P.112 ▶ SÝNDAGMA & AROUND ▼

Hills and views

Athens is dotted with hills and surrounded by mountains, almost all of which offer great **views** and the opportunity to escape the clamour of the city for a while. Inevitably, the Acropolis seems to find its way into every photo, but there are fine **cityscapes** to be enjoyed in other directions too. The Acropolis itself offers good views of the city, while Lykavitós is the other classic viewpoint – with the added advantage of a walk through elegant Kolonáki and a funicular to get you to the top. On the fringes of the city, the **mountains** of Imittós and Párnitha are surprisingly rugged – making them excellent hiking territory.

The Acropolis

Great views as you look northeast from the Acropolis, with Pláka below, Sýndagma and the city centre behind, and Lykavitós in the background.

▸ P.51 ▸ THE ACROPOLIS

Filopáppou

Filopáppou hill, romantically known in antiquity as the Hill of the Muses, is topped by a grandiose monument to the Roman senator after whom it is named.

P.82 THISSÍO, GÁZI & ÁNO PETRÁLONA

Lófos tou Stréfi

Stréfi hill is little visited and offers a quiet escape from the streets of surrounding Exarhía.

P.98 THE ARCHEOLOGICAL MUSEUM EXÁRHIA & NEÁPOLI

Lykavitós

From the top, Athens is laid out before you in all directions – on a clear day you can see as far as the mountains of the Peloponnese.

P.104 KOLONÁKI AND LYKAVITÓS HILL

The Pnyx

The remains of the ancient Athenian assembly stand at the summit of the Hill of the Pnyx, looking out over Pireás to the sea.

P.82 THE ARCHEOLOGICAL MUSEUM EXÁRHIA & NEÁPOLI

Green Athens

At first sight Athens is not a green city, but it has its moments. The citizens decorate their balconies with potted plants and shrubs, while in the older quarters **bougainvillea** covers many houses. In spring, flowers try to blossom everywhere – **archeological sites** and the steeper slopes of the **hills** are ideal breeding grounds. At the very heart of the city, the **National Gardens** offer almost tropical luxuriance, while as soon as you leave the city limits, nature reasserts itself immediately, whether in the **mountains**, the **coast** or the nearby **islands**.

Égina

The island of Égina, less than an hour by hydrofoil from Athens, is famed for its many green orchards bearing pistachios.

▸P.147 ▸ FURTHER AFIELD ▲

The National Gardens

Part formally laid out, part distinctly overgrown, the National Gardens make for a refreshing, shady escape from the summer heat.

▸P.114 ▸ SÝNDAGMA & AROUND ▲

Ruins in spring

Even in the heart of Athens, in springtime flowers burst through and adorn the many ancient remains.

▸ P.51 ▸ THE ACROPOLIS ▼

Lykavitós

The lower slopes of Lykavitós and many of the city's other hills are covered in pine trees and succulents.

▸ P.104 ▸ KOLONÁKI & LYKAVITÓS HILL ▲

Mount Párnitha

Less than an hour by bus from the city centre, Mount Párnitha is remarkably wild, with a fabulous variety of alpine flowers in spring.

▸ P.137 ▸ ATTICA ▼

Restaurants and tavernas

Athens has a huge variety of restaurants and tavernas. The atmosphere is invariably relaxed, though the city does have its share of fancy places. There's virtually every type of **cuisine** too, but the vast majority of places, and the ones most frequented by locals, remain no-frills **tavernas**. Most menus are simple, but you can rely on good-quality, fresh ingredients: if you're not sure about the menu, you can often go into the kitchen and see what's on offer. A typically Greek way to eat is to order a selection of small dishes – ***mezédhes*** – to share. Locals generally eat late: 2–3.30pm for lunch, 9–11pm for dinner. Away from the touristy areas, you may find restaurants deserted if you go much earlier than this.

Zidhoron

In the heart of trendy Psyrrí, Zidhoron is a modern take on a traditional *mezedhopolío*.

▸P.79 ▸ MONASTIRÁKI & PSYRRÍ ▲

Koukáki

An excellent eating locale just outside the centre.

▸P121 ▸ METS, PANGRÁTI & KOUKÁKI ▲

Pláka

Most Athens restaurants have a terrace, courtyard or stretch of pavement on which tables are set up outside in summer. The pedestrian streets of Pláka provide a particularly atmospheric setting.

▸P.68 ▸ PLÁKA ▼

Taverna music

Evening performances of traditional Greek music are common, and while often rather touristy they are occasionally great.

▸P.78 ▸ MONASTIRÁKI & PSYRRÍ ▼

Taverna Damingos

A basement taverna that's still going strong into its third century.

▸P.68 ▸ PLÁKA ▲

Áno Petrálona

Away from the touristy central districts, neighbourhoods such as Áno Petrálona generally offer more authentic menus and a more local atmosphere.

▸P.85 ▸ THISSÍO, GÁZI & ÁNO PETRÁLONA ▲

Cafés and bars

There seems to be a café on every corner in Athens, most of which open from mid-morning till late in the evening. They're an essential part of the social fabric of the city, always full of groups of people chatting (on their mobiles if not to each other), smoking and drinking. Join them over a **Greek coffee** or the quintessential summer drink, a ***frappé***: iced instant coffee, whipped to a froth. If you fancy a cold beer, you can have that in a café too – many effectively become **bars** in the evening, when they turn down the lights and turn up the music. Places that describe themselves as bars, with only a few exceptions, are much fancier and more expensive.

Brettos

Backlit bottles decorate Brettos, a perennial Pláka favourite that's a liquor store by day and bar at night.

▸P.67 ▸ PLÁKA ▲

Psyrrí

By night, Psyrrí buzzes with some of the city's trendiest bars and restaurants, while by day it's a relaxing place for a coffee.

▸ P.79 ▸ MONASTIRÁKI & PSYRRÍ ▾

Exárhia

An alternative feel prevails at the cafés and bars in this bohemian district.

▸ P.100 ▸ THE ARCHEOLOGICAL MUSEUM, EXÁRHIA & NEÁPOLI ▾

Platía Filomoússou Eterías

Competing cafés and restaurants in the heart of Pláka.

▸ P.67 ▸ PLÁKA ▲

Skholarhio

This traditional *ouzerí* in Pláka serves excellent *mezédhes*.

▸ P.69 ▸ PLÁKA ▾

Music and entertainment

To see the best live **traditional Greek music**, perhaps surprisingly you need to visit during the winter months, as in the summer many musicians are off touring the country.

This is also when the major **ballet** and **drama** performances are staged, and the **sporting calendar** is at its busiest. The summer, however, is the festival season, and most important of all is the June-to-September **Hellenic Festival** of dance, music and ancient drama, with many of its performances staged in the ancient theatres of Herodes Atticus and Epidaurus. There are also annual **rock**, **jazz** and **blues** events at this time, and you may see big international tours at one of the outdoor venues.

Mégaro Mousikís

The city's major concert hall, the Mégaro Mousikís, hosts prestigious performances all year-round.

▸P.169 ▸ ESSENTIALS

Rebétika

Traditional music falls broadly into two categories: *rebétika*, the drugs-and-outcast music brought to Athens by Greeks from Asia Minor in the early twentieth century; and *dhimotiká*, traditional folk music.

▸P.94 ▸ PLATÍA OMONÍAS & AROUND

Street music

The pedestrianization of much of the centre has allowed street performers and traders to thrive; the approach to the Acropolis is particularly good for seeing buskers.

▸P.53 ▸ THE ACROPOLIS ▲

Football

There are three major football clubs in Athens: Panathinaikós, Olympiakós and AEK; the atmosphere on match days is intense.

▸P.170 ▸ ESSENTIALS ▶

Lykavitós Theatre

The theatre perched atop Lykavitós is a spectacular venue. Many of the city's major rock events are staged here.

▸P.105 ▸ KOLONÁKI & LYKAVITÓS HILL ▼

Nightlife

Clubs and dance bars are hugely popular in Athens, and often extremely sophisticated. Downtown, the hottest action is in the **Psyrrí** and **Gázi** areas, but in summer many close down and decamp to a string of hangar-like places on the coastal strip from **Pireás** to **Várkiza**. Expect the unexpected: most play recent hits, but don't be surprised if the sound shifts to Greek or belly-dancing music towards the end of the night. The **gay scene** in Athens is mostly very discreet, but there is an increasing number of clubs and bars; Gázi is the hottest new area, while more established places are mostly in Kolonáki or off Syngroú Avenue.

Kolonáki

Kolonáki has a fair spread of clubs, which tend to be generally more upmarket than those in Psyrrí or Gázi.

▸P.111 ▸ KOLONÁKI & LYKAVITÓS HILL ▲

Bee Bar

Typically cool designer bar in Psyrrí, a great place to meet up at the beginning of the evening, or to chill out in later.

▸P.79 ▸ MONASTIRÁKI & PSRRÍ ▲

Beach clubs

Beachside clubs and bars open up in summer to cater to the clubbers seeking the cooler climes of the coast.

▸P.132 ▸ SUBURBAN ATHENS ▼

Clubbing

Expect a hefty bill if you join the clubbing crowd, but at least the admission price usually includes your first drink.

▸P.87 ▸ THISSÍO, GÁZI & ÁNO PETRÁLONA ▼

Live bands

The local rock scene is small but interesting – you can expect anything from rock to reggae to blues.

▸P101 ▸ THE ARCHEOLOGICAL MUSEUM, EXÁRHIA & NEÁPOLI ▲

Markets and shopping

Shopping in Athens is decidedly schizophrenic. On the one hand, the **bazaar** area is an extraordinary jumble of little specialist shops and stalls, while almost every neighbourhood still hosts a weekly street **market**. On the other, the upmarket shopping areas of the city centre, and the **malls** and fashion emporia of the ritzier suburbs, are as glossy and expensive as any in Europe. The **food halls** of the central market and the picturesque **flower market** nearby are particularly worthwhile, while if you're into trawling through junk, don't miss the Sunday morning **flea markets** in Monastiráki and Pireás.

Street markets

Street markets held across the city are great places to stock up on picnic fare and get a taste of local Athens.

▸P.170 ▸ ESSENTIALS

Odhós Ermoú

Ermoú, off Sýndagma square, is one of the prime downtown shopping streets, home to department stores and high-street labels.

▸P.70 ▸ MONASTIRÁKI & PSYRRÍ ▼

The fish market

Seafood and fish play a big part in the Athenian diet, and at the bustling fish market you'll see residents and taverna owners alike browsing the catch.

▸P.88 ▸ PLATÍAS OMONÍAS & AROUND ▼

Monastiráki flea market

Experience the Sunday morning buzz in the streets around Monastiráki.

▸P.74 ▸ MONASTIRÁKI & PSYRRÍ ▲

Períptero kiosks

Handy for anything from newspapers to cold drinks, tobacco and any manner of essentials, kiosks are found on every corner and stay open all hours. Several in Omónia specialize in the foreign press.

▸P.88 ▸ PLATÍAS OMONÍAS & AROUND ▼

Orthodox Athens

Greece remains a deeply traditional and for the most part culturally homogeneous society, and over ninety-five percent of the population belongs to the **Greek Orthodox Church**. For all its surface modernity, Athens is no exception. The Orthodox church plays a significant part in most people's lives: ceremonies like baptisms, weddings and funerals are very important, and the **festivals** of the church calendar – Easter above all – are celebrated with gusto. Name days – celebrating the saint after whom you are named – are more significant than birthdays.

Icon shops

Icons, from cheap reproductions aimed at the tourist market to expensive and exquisite copies are sold everywhere: some of the best are found in the religious artefact shops around Platía Mitrópoleos.

▸P.76▸ MONASTIRÁKI & PSYRRÍ ▲

Platía Mitrópoleos

The square itself is more of a draw than the cathedral here, but there has been a church on this site for centuries

▸P.75 ▸ MONASTIRÁKI & PSYRRÍ ▲

Baptism ceremonies

Events like baptisms bring out a vast, extended family – all of whom can expect lavish hospitality.

▸P.70 ▸ MONASTIRÁKI & PSYRRÍ ▼

Historic icons

When you've had your fill of browsing the icon shops, check out their historic predecessors at the Byzantine and Christian museum.

▸P.106 ▸ KOLONÁKI AND LYKAVITÓS HILL ▼

Athens on foot

Central Athens is compact enough to be able to walk almost anywhere. One of the lasting legacies of the run up to 2004 Olympics is undoubtedly be the network of **pedestrian streets** that transformed the centre of town. Quite apart from the pleasure of being able to witness the ancient sites from a traffic-free environment, pedestrianization, together with the extension of the metro and other public transport initiatives have started to have an effect on Athens' critical pollution problems.

Apostólou Pávlou

Modern sculpture adorns the pedestrianized street that overlooks the Agora and Acropolis.

P.80 THISSÍO, GÁZI & ÁNO PETRÁLONA

Odhós Ermoú

Ermoú is a wonderfully traffic-free route from Sýndagma down the Monastiráki.

P.70 MONASTIRÁKI & PSYRRÍ

Kolonáki

The upper reaches of Kolonáki climb steeply towards Lykavitós hill – it's easiest to take the funicular up and walk down.

▸ P.102 ▸ KOLONÁKI & LYKAVITÓS HILL ▼

Odhós Adhrianoú

From Thissío metro all the way through Pláka, Adhrianoú is lined with bustling cafés and shops.

▸ P.75 ▸ MONASTIRÁKI & PSYRRÍ ▲

Dhionysíou Areopayítou

A relaxed, traffic-free street on the south side of the Acropolis, passing the Herodes Atticus Theatre.

▸ P.53 ▸ THE ACROPOLIS ▼

Seaside Athens and island escapes

Athens is surrounded by the sea, and the Greek nation has a seafaring tradition going back to Classical times. There are some great **beaches** in easy reach, though on summer weekends they're packed to capacity. At many of the best you pay for entry, allowing you to use a range of facilities from loungers to watersports. More adventurously, from the port of **Pireás** you can get a ferry to one of a number of nearby **islands**, escaping in just a couple of hours (half that if you take a hydrofoil) to an entirely different world.

Náfplio

The beautiful old town of Náfplio, with its picturesque castles, attracts plenty of weekending Athenians, ensuring lively nightlife to go with the sights.

▸P.146 ▸ FURTHER AFIELD ▲

Beach at Vouliagméni

Vouliagméni has some of the most attractive and exclusive beaches on the developed strip south of the city.

▸P128 ▸ SUBURBAN ATHENS ▲

Póros

Picturesque Póros lies in close proximity to the mainland, ensuring a steady stream of customers for its fine waterfront restaurants and cafés.

▸P.148 ▸ FURTHER AFIELD ▼

Temple of Afaia, Égina

The rural island of Égina seems another world – the serene Temple of Afaia can be reached by a good local bus service.

▸P.147 ▸ FURTHER AFIELD ▲

Ferries from Pireás

Part of the magic of visiting the islands is the journey itself; an impressive array of ferries, catamarans and hydrofoils offer a smooth crossing as they run between the bustling port and the islands.

▸P.127 ▸ SUBURBAN ATHENS ▼

Out of Athens

Attica, the province surrounding Athens, has numerous attractions beyond the obvious ones offered by its beaches: above all, the important outposts of Classical Athens, made all the more appealing now by their rural isolation. Further out, some of the great sites, including **Delphi** and **Mycenae**, are an easy day-trip. The **mountains**, with their traditional villages, walking and even skiing opportunities, are yet another alternative.

Mycenae

The discovery of Mycenae in the late nineteenth century was a seminal event in Greek archeology, proving that Homer and the stories of ancient, pre-Classical civilizations were not mere myth.

▸ P.147 ▸ FURTHER AFIELD

Rhamnous

Ancient Rhamnous is little visited, but the site enjoys a spectacular location overlooking the island of Évvia.

▸ P.136 ▸ ATTICA

Delphi

Delphi, home of the Delphic Oracle, was thought by the ancient Greeks to be the centre of the earth. It's still among the most impressive of all ancient sites.

▸P.141 ▸ FURTHER AFIELD ▲

Eleusis

The Sanctuary of Demeter at Eleusis – accessible by city bus from Athens – was one of the most important in the ancient world.

▸P.137 ▸ ATTICA ▼

Temple of Poseidon

Cape Soúnio and the beautiful temple that stands at its tip have long been a landmark for sailors approaching Athens.

▸P.133 ▸ ATTICA ▲

Mount Parnitha

Looking out from the ancient fortress of Phyle, just an hour from the centre of Athens, the unspoilt nature of Mount Parnitha is readily apparent.

▸P137 ▸ ATTICA ▼

Places

Places

The Acropolis

The rock of the Acropolis, crowned by the dramatic ruins of the Parthenon, is one of the archetypal images of Western culture. The first time you see it, rising above the traffic or from a distant hill, is extraordinary: foreign and yet utterly familiar. The Parthenon temple was always intended to be a landmark, and was famous throughout the ancient world. Yet even in their wildest dreams its creators could hardly have imagined that the ruins would come to symbolize the emergence of Western civilization – nor that, two-and-a-half millennia on, it would attract some three million tourists a year.

The Acropolis's natural setting, a steep-sided, flat-topped crag of limestone rising abruptly a hundred metres from its surroundings, has made it the focus of the city during every phase of its development. Easily defensible and with plentiful water, its initial attractions are obvious – even now, with no function apart from tourism, it is the undeniable heart of the city, around which everything else clusters, glimpsed at almost every turn.

Crowds at the Acropolis can be horrendous – to avoid the worst, come very early or late in the day. The peak rush usually comes in late morning, when coach tours congregate before moving on to lunch elsewhere.

The sites included in this chapter fall within one of three separate fenced areas: the summit of the Acropolis, which includes the Parthenon itself, the Propylaia – the gateway through which the ancient sanctuary was entered – the Acropolis Museum, and other temples including the Erectheion and the Temple of Athena Nike; the South Slope

▼ PARTHENON

Acropolis tickets and opening times

A joint ticket (€12; free to under-18s and EU students; €6 for non-EU students and EU citizens over 65; free on public holidays and Sundays Nov–March) covers the Acropolis, Ancient Agora and South Slope, plus the Roman Forum, Kerameikos and the Temple of Olympian Zeus. The smaller sites also offer individual tickets, but only the joint one is valid for the summit of the Acropolis, so if you visit any of the others first, be sure to buy the multiple ticket or you simply end up paying twice; it can be used over four days, although there doesn't seem to be any way of indicating when it was issued.

The Acropolis itself is **open** every day April–Sept 8am–7pm, Oct–March 8am–4.30pm. The South Slope (individual entry €2) and Ancient Agora (individual entry €4) are open daily April–Sept 8am–7pm, Oct–March 8.30am–3pm.

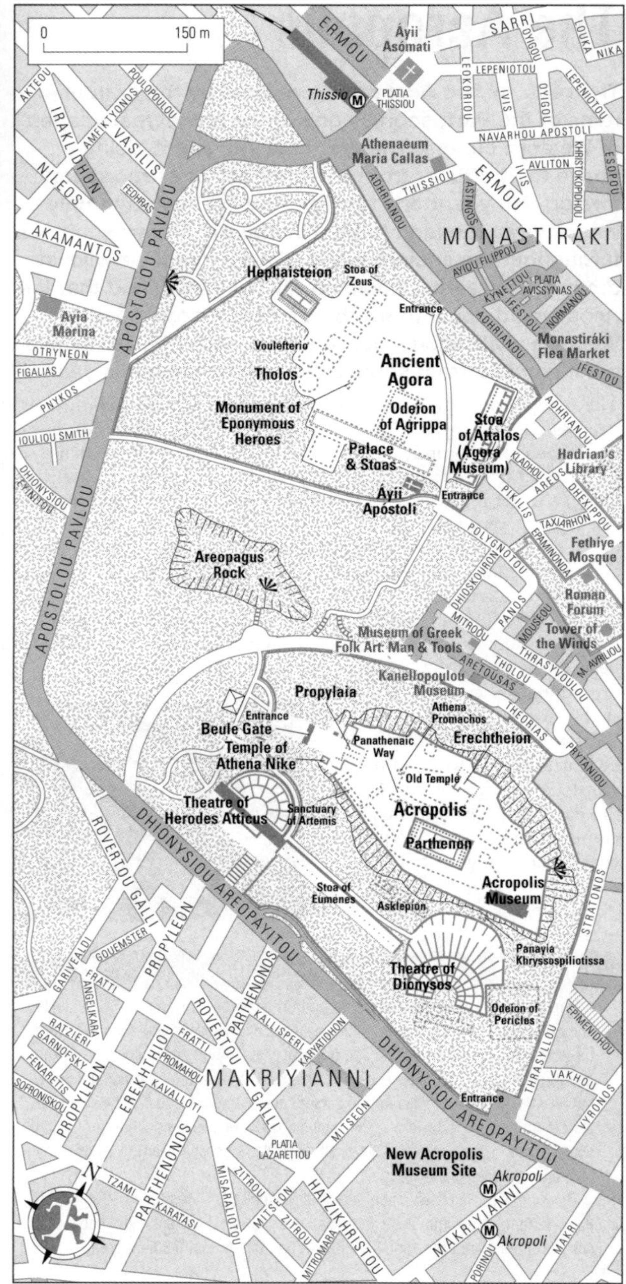

0 150 m
Áyii Asómati
Thissio
PLATIA THISSIOU
Athenaeum Maria Callas
MONASTIRÁKI
Hephaisteion
Stoa of Zeus
Entrance
Vouleftirio
Tholos
Ancient Agora
Monument of Eponymous Heroes
Odeion of Agrippa
Stoa of Attalos (Agora Museum)
Palace & Stoas
Áyii Apóstoli
Entrance
Monastiráki Flea Market
Hadrian's Library
Fethiye Mosque
Roman Forum
Tower of the Winds
Areopagus Rock
Museum of Greek Folk Art: Man & Tools
Kanellopoulou Museum
Ayia Marina
Propylaia
Entrance
Beule Gate
Temple of Athena Nike
Athena Promachos
Erechtheion
Panathenaic Way
Old Temple
Theatre of Herodes Atticus
Sanctuary of Artemis
Acropolis
Parthenon
Acropolis Museum
Stoa of Eumenes
Asklepion
Panayia Khryssospiliotissa
Theatre of Dionysos
Odeion of Pericles
Entrance
MAKRIYIÁNNI
PLATIA LAZARETTOU
New Acropolis Museum Site
Akropoli
Akropoli
APOSTOLOU PAVLOU
DHIONYSIOU AREOPAYITOU
ERMOU
ADHRIANOU

Approaches to the Acropolis

The sites are ringed by a pedestrian walkway, allowing views of the Parthenon to be appreciated from almost every angle. You may get a little lost among the jumble of alleys in Pláka, but the rock itself is always there to guide you. The Acropolis itself can be entered only from the west, where there's a big coach park at the bottom of the hill.

On foot, the most common approach to the ruins is from the northwest corner of Pláka, on a path that extends above Odhós Dhioskoúron where it joins Theorías. You can also approach from the south, where pedestrianized Dhionysíou Areopayítou (Metro Akropoli) offers access to the South Slope; from the north via the Ancient Agora (entrance on Adhrianoú; Metro Monastiráki); or, slightly further but repaid with excellent views of both Agora and Acropolis, from Thissío along traffic-free Apostólou Pávlou (Metro Thissío).

with its two great theatres; and the Ancient Agora.

There are no shops or restaurants within the Acropolis area, although you can buy water and sandwiches, guidebooks, postcards and so on from a couple of stands near the Beule Gate. There's also a handy branch of Everest right opposite Akropoli metro station (at the corner of Mariyiánni and Dhiakoú) and plenty of similar places around Monastiráki metro. If you want to sit down, there are cafés and tavernas nearby in almost every direction: see Pláka (p.68), Monastiráki (p.77), Makriyánni (p.121) and Thissío (p.85).

The Propylaia

Main Acropolis site. Today, as throughout history, the Propylaia are the gateway to the Acropolis. In Classical times the road extended along a steep ramp to this monumental double-gatehouse; the modern path makes a more gradual, zigzagging ascent, passing first through an arched Roman entrance, the Beule Gate, added in the third century AD.

The Propylaia were constructed by Mnesikles from 437–432 BC, and their axis and proportions aligned to balance the recently completed Parthenon. They were built from the same marble as the temple, and in grandeur and architectural achievement are almost as impressive. The ancient Athenians, awed by the fact that such wealth and craftsmanship should be used for a purely secular building, ranked this as their most prestigious monument.

Walking through the gateway, which would originally have had great wooden doors, is your only chance to enter any of the ancient buildings atop the Acropolis. To the left of the central hall (which before Venetian bombardment supported a great coffered roof, painted blue and gilded with stars), the Pinakotheke was an early art gallery, exhibiting paintings of Homeric subjects by

▼ PROPYLAIA

The development of the Acropolis

The rocky Acropolis was home to one of the earliest known settlements in Greece, its slopes inhabited by a **Neolithic** community around 5000 BC. In **Mycenaean** times it was fortified with Cyclopean walls (parts of which can still be seen), enclosing a royal palace and temples to the goddess Athena. By the ninth century BC, the Acropolis had become the heart of Athens, the first Greek city-state, sheltering its principal public buildings.

Most of the substantial remains seen today date from the **fifth century BC** or later, by which time the buildings here were purely religious. The entire area was reconstructed in 449 BC, following its sacking during the Persian Wars. This vast project, coinciding with the Golden Age of Classical Athens, was masterminded by **Pericles** and carried out under the general direction of the architect and sculptor **Pheidias**. It was completed in an incredibly short time: the Parthenon itself took only ten years to finish.

The monuments survived barely altered for close to a thousand years, until in the reign of Emperor Justinian the temples were converted to **Christian** places of worship. Over the following centuries, the uses became secular as well as religious, and embellishments increased, gradually obscuring the Classical designs. Fifteenth-century Italian princes held court in the Propylaia, and the same quarters were later used by the **Turks** as their commander's headquarters and as a powder magazine. The Parthenon underwent similar changes from Greek to Roman temple, from Byzantine church to Frankish cathedral, before several centuries of use as a Turkish mosque. The Erechtheion, with its graceful female figures, saw service as a harem.

The Acropolis buildings finally fell victim to war, blown up during successive attempts by the Venetians to oust the Turks. In 1684 the Turks demolished the Temple of Athena Nike to gain a brief tactical advantage. Three years later the Venetians, laying siege to the hill, ignited a Turkish gunpowder magazine in the Parthenon, in the process blasting off its roof and starting a fire that raged for two days and nights.

The process of stripping down to the bare ruins seen today was completed by souvenir hunters and the efforts of the first archeologists (see p.56).

The fate of the buildings since has been little happier. After Independence, Greek archeologists cleared the Turkish village that had developed around the Parthenon-mosque and did work intended to preserve the structures: in the long run, though, much of this proved destructive. Meanwhile, earthquakes have dislodged the foundations; generations of feet have slowly worn down surfaces; and, more recently, sulphur dioxide deposits, caused by vehicle and industrial pollution, have been turning the marble to dust.

Since a 1975 report predicted the collapse of the Parthenon, visitors have been barred from its actual precinct, and a major, long-term restoration scheme of the entire Acropolis embarked upon. With the work completed as a result of the 2004 Olympics, the Acropolis would be free of scaffolding and reconstruction work for the first time in decades.

Polygnotus. The wing to the right is much smaller, as Mnesikles's original design incorporated ground sacred to the Goddess of Victory and the premises had to be adapted as a waiting room for her shrine – the Temple of Athena Nike.

The Panathenaic Way

Main Acropolis site. The Panathenaic Way was the route along which the great procession for ancient Athens' Panathenaic Festival, in honour of the city's patron goddess Athena, passed every four years.

The procession wound right through the Classical city from the gates now in the Kerameikos site (p.83) via the Propylaia to the Parthenon and, finally, the Erectheion. One of the best-preserved stretches of the ancient route, which was of course used as a road between festivals too, can be seen just inside the Propylaia. Here you can make out grooves cut for footholds in the rock and, to either side, niches for innumerable statues and offerings. In Classical times it ran past a ten-metre-high bronze statue of *Athena Promachos* (Athena the Champion), whose base can just about be made out. Athena's spear and helmet were said to be visible to sailors approaching from as far away as Sounío. The statue was moved to Constantinople in Byzantine times and later destroyed.

The Temple of Athena Nike

Main Acropolis site. Simple and elegant, the Temple of Athena Nike stands on a precipitous platform overlooking the port of Pireás and the Saronic Gulf. The temple's frieze depicts the Athenians' victory over the Persians at Plateia. A relief from inside the temple, *Victory Adjusting her Sandal*, is now one of the star exhibits in the Acropolis Museum. It was from this site that in myth King Aegeus maintained a vigil for the return of his son Theseus after slaying the Minotaur on Crete – and where Aegeus threw himself to his death, mistakenly believing Theseus had perished.

Amazingly, the whole temple was demolished by the Turks, who used its material for a gun emplacement, and reconstructed from its original blocks two hundred years later. The same process was undertaken in the run-up to the 2004 Olympic Games – the temple was temporarily dismantled and its pieces taken away for restoration and cleaning.

The best views of the temple are from inside the Acropolis, to the right after passing through the Propylaia. Here also are the scant remains of a Sanctuary of Brauronian Artemis. Although its function remains obscure, it is known that the precinct once housed a colossal bronze representation of the Wooden Horse of Troy. More noticeable is a nearby stretch of Mycenaean wall (running parallel to the Propylaia) that was incorporated into the Classical design.

The Parthenon

Main Acropolis site. The Parthenon was the first great building in Pericles' scheme, intended as a new sanctuary for Athena and a home for her cult image – a colossal wooden statue of *Athena Polias* (Athena of the City) overlaid with ivory and gold plating, with precious gems as eyes and

▲ PARTHENON FRIEZE

The Parthenon Marbles

The controversy over the so-called **Elgin Marbles** has its origin in the activities of Western looters at the start of the nineteenth century. Chief among these were the French ambassador Fauvel, gathering antiquities for the Louvre, and the British ambassador **Lord Elgin**. Elgin obtained permission from the Turks to erect scaffolding, excavate and remove stones with inscriptions. He interpreted this concession as a licence to make off with almost all of the bas-reliefs from the Parthenon's frieze, most of its pedimental structures and a caryatid from the Erechtheion – all of which he later sold to the British Museum. There were perhaps justifications for Elgin's action at the time – not least the Turks' tendency to use Parthenon stones in their limekilns, and possible further ravages of war – though it was controversial even then.

The Greeks hope that the long-awaited completion of the new Acropolis Museum (see p.59) will create the perfect opportunity for the British Museum to bow to pressure and return the marbles. But despite a campaign begun by Greek actress and culture minister Melina Mercouri in the early 1980s, there is so far little sign of that happening.

an ivory gorgon death's-head on her breast. The sculpture has long been lost, but numerous later copies exist (including a fine Roman one in the National Archeological Museum). Despite the statue, the Parthenon never rivalled the Erechtheion in sanctity, and its role tended to remain that of treasury and artistic showcase.

Originally the Parthenon's columns were brightly painted and it was decorated with the finest sculpture of the Classical age, depicting the Panathenaic procession, the birth of Athena and the struggles of Greeks to overcome giants, Amazons and centaurs – also brightly coloured. Of these, the best surviving examples are in the British Museum in London (see box above); the Acropolis Museum has others, but the greater part of the pediments, along with the central columns and the *cella*, were destroyed by the Venetian bombardment in 1687.

To achieve the Parthenon's exceptional harmony of design, its architect, Iktinos, used every trick known to the Doric order of architecture. Every ratio – length to width, width to height, and even such relationships as the distances between the columns and their diameter – is constant, while any possible appearance of disproportion is corrected by meticulous mathematics and craftsmanship.

The Erechtheion

Main Acropolis site. The Erechtheion was the last of the great works of Pericles to be completed. Both Athena and the city's old patron, Poseidon (known here as Erechtheus), were worshipped here, in the most revered of the ancient temples. The site is the oldest on the Acropolis, home to the original Mycenaean palace. It was here, according to myth, that Athena and Poseidon wrangled for possession of Athens. A contest was held to decide their rival claims, judged by their fellow Olympian gods. At the touch of Athena's spear, the first ever olive tree sprang from the ground, while Poseidon summoned forth a spring of sea water. Athena won, and became patron of the city.

Today, the sacred objects within are long gone, but the series of elegant Ionic porticoes survive, the north one with a particularly fine decorated doorway and frieze of blue Eleusinian marble. By far the most striking feature, however, is the famous Porch of the Caryatids, whose columns form the tunics of six tall maidens. The ones *in situ* are, sadly, replacements. Five of the originals are in the Acropolis Museum, while a sixth was looted by Elgin, who also removed a column and other purely architectural features – they're replaced here by casts in a different colour marble.

The Acropolis Museum

Main Acropolis site. April–Sept Mon 11am–7pm, Tues–Sun 8am–7pm; Oct–March Mon 10am–3pm, Tues–Sun 8.30am–3pm. Placed discreetly on a level below that of the main monuments, the Acropolis Museum contains virtually all of the portable objects removed from the site since 1834.

▼ ACROPOLIS MUSEUM

Labelling is fairly basic, so to explore in detail a supplementary guide is useful, though it's also easy to eavesdrop on the many tour guides passing through – indeed, usually it's impossible to avoid doing so.

In the first rooms to the left of the vestibule are fragments of sculptures from the Old Temple of Athena (seventh to sixth century BC), whose traces of paint give a good impression of the vivid colours that were used in temple decoration. Further on is the Moschophoros, a painted marble statue of a young man carrying a sacrificial calf, dated 570 BC and one of the earliest examples of Greek art in marble. Room 4 displays one of the chief treasures of the building, a unique collection of Korai, or statues of maidens. The progression in style, from the simply contoured Doric clothing to the more elegant and voluminous Ionic designs, is fascinating; the figures' smiles also change subtly, becoming increasingly loose and natural.

The pieces of the Parthenon frieze in Room 8 were buried in the explosion that destroyed the Parthenon, thereby escaping the clutches of Lord Elgin. This room also contains a graceful and fluid sculpture, known as Iy Sandalízoussa, which depicts Athena Nike adjusting her sandal. Finally, in the last room are four authentic and semi-eroded caryatids from the Erechtheion, displayed behind a glass screen in a carefully rarefied atmosphere.

Theatre of Dionysos

South slope site. The Theatre of Dionysos is one of the most evocative locations in the city. Here were hosted the first performances of the masterpieces of Aeschylus, Sophocles, Euripides and Aristophanes; it was also the venue in Classical times for the annual festival of tragic drama, where each Greek citizen would take his turn as member of the chorus. The theatre could hold some 17,000 spectators – considerably more than Herodes Atticus's 5000–6000 seats; twenty of the original 64 tiers of seats survive. Most notable are the great marble thrones in the front row, each inscribed with the name of an official of the festival or of an important priest; in the middle sat the priest of Dionysos and on his right the representative of the Delphic Oracle. At the rear of the stage along the Roman *bema* (rostrum) are reliefs of episodes in the life of Dionysos. Sadly, this area is roped off to protect the stage-floor mosaic, a magnificent diamond of multicoloured marble best seen from the seats above.

Around the Theatre

South slope site. The dominant structure on the south side of the Acropolis – much more immediately obvious even than the Theatre of Dionysos – is the second-century Roman **Herodes Atticus Theatre** (Odeion of Herodes Atticus). This has been extensively restored for performances of music and Classical drama during the summer festival (see p.170). Unfortunately, it's open only for shows; at other times you'll have to be content with spying over the wall.

Between the two theatres lie the foundations of the **Stoa of Eumenes**, originally a massive colonnade of stalls erected in the second century BC. Above the stoa extend the ruins of the **Asklepion**, a sanctuary devoted to the healing god Asklepios and built around a sacred spring. Today, it's a pleasantly peaceful spot, shaded by cypress trees; the most obvious remains are of a Byzantine church of the doctor-saints Kosmas and Damian. Follow the steps above the Theatre of Dionysos, then a path to the right, and you'll come to a vast grotto, converted perhaps a millennium ago into the chapel of Panayía Khryssospiliótissa; it's worth a look for the setting rather than the faded iconography inside.

▲ THEATRE OF DIONYSOS

The New Acropolis Museum

Leóforos Dhionysíou Areopayítou, opposite the South Slope site. After years of delays, work on the new Acropolis Museum finally began in 2003. This is set to be stunning: the top storey is an all-glass affair designed to house the Parthenon Marbles (those already in the Acropolis Museum, plus the restored Elgin Marbles), with a direct view up to the Parthenon itself. Downstairs, the rest of the contents of the current Acropolis Museum will be far better displayed than they can be now, and there's also a raised, part-glass floor, added to the design to preserve and display remains of early Christian Athens, discovered during building work.

The Areopagus

Immediately below the entrance to the Acropolis. Slippery, rock-hewn stairs ascend the low, unfenced hill of the Areopagus, the site of the Council of Nobles and the Judicial Court under the aristocratic rule of ancient Athens. During the Classical period the court lost its powers of government to the Assembly (held on the Pnyx), but it remained the court of criminal justice, dealing primarily with cases of homicide. In myth it was also the rock (*pagos*) where Ares, God of War, was tried for the murder of one of Poseidon's sons. Aeschylus used this setting in *The Eumenides* for the trial of Orestes, who stood accused of murdering his mother Clytemnestra.

The Persians camped here during their siege of the Acropolis in 480 BC, and in the Roman era Saint Paul preached the "Sermon on an Unknown God" on the hill, winning amongst his converts Dionysius "the Areopagite", who became the city's patron saint. Today, there's little left on the ground, and, historic associations apart, the Areopagus is notable mainly for the views, especially down over the Agora and towards the ancient cemetery of Kerameikós.

The Ancient Agora

Ancient Agora site. The Agora or market was the heart of ancient Athenian city life from as early as 3000 BC. Today, the site is an extensive and rather confusing jumble of ruins, dating from various stages of building between the sixth century BC and the fifth century AD. As well as the marketplace, the Agora was the chief meeting place of the city, where orators held forth, business was discussed and gossip exchanged. It was also the first home of the democratic assembly before that shifted to the Pnyx, and continued to be its meeting place when cases of ostracism were discussed for most of the Classical period.

Originally the Agora was a rectangle, divided diagonally by the Panathenaic Way and enclosed by temples, administrative buildings, and long porticoed *stoas* (arcades of shops). In the centre was an open space, defined by boundary stones.

The best overview of the site is from the exceptionally well-preserved Hephaisteion, or **Temple of Hephaistos**, which overlooks the rest of the site from the west. An observation point in front of it has a plan showing the buildings as they were in 150 AD, and the various remains laid out in front of you make a lot more sense with this to help (there are similar plans at the entrances). The temple, sometimes known as the

▲ STOA OF ATTALOS

Thisseion (the exploits of Theseus are depicted on the frieze), is dedicated to Hephaistos, patron of black-smiths and metalworkers. It was one of the earliest buildings of Pericles' programme, but also one of the least known – perhaps because it lacks the curvature and "lightness" of the Parthenon's design. The barrel-vaulted roof dates from a Byzantine conversion into the church of Saint George.

The other church on the site – that of **Áyii Apóstoli** (the Holy Apostles), by the south entrance – is worth a look as you wander among the extensive foundations of the other Agora buildings. Inside are fragments of fresco, exposed during restoration of the eleventh-century shrine.

Stoa of Attalos

Ancient Agora site. For some background to the Agora, head for the Museum, housed in the magnificent Stoa of Attalos. The reconstruction of the *stoa* was undertaken by the American School of Archeology in Athens between 1953 and 1956. It is, in every respect except colour, an entirely faithful reconstruction of the original; lacking colour or no, the building is spectacular. Sadly, it doesn't deliver inside – the display is small and old-fashioned, with labels that look as if they've been here since it opened in 1957. The bulk of what you see is pottery and coins from the sixth to the fourth century BC, plus some early Geometric grave offerings – including red-figure dishes depicting athletes, musicians and minor deities, together with an oil flask in the form of a kneeling boy. Look out for the *ostraka*, or shards of pottery, with names written on them. At annual assemblies of the citizens, these *ostraka* would be handed in, and the individual with most votes banished, or "ostracized", from the city for ten years.

Pláka

The largely pedestrianized area of Pláka, with its narrow lanes and stepped alleys climbing towards the Acropolis, is arguably the most attractive part of Athens, and certainly the most popular with visitors. In addition to a scattering of ancient sites and various offbeat and enjoyable museums, it offers glimpses of an older Athens, refreshingly at odds with the concrete blocks of the metropolis.

Although surrounded by huge, traffic-choked avenues, Pláka itself is a welcome escape, its narrow streets offering no through-routes for traffic even where you are allowed to drive. Nineteenth-century houses, some grand, some humble, can be seen everywhere, their gateways opening onto verdant courtyards overlooked by wooden verandahs.

With scores of cafés and restaurants to fill the time between museums and sites, and streets lined with touristy shops, it's an enjoyable place to wander. The main disadvantage is price – things are noticeably more expensive in Pláka than in much of the rest of the city.

Museum of Greek Folk Art

Kydhathinéon 17. Tues–Sun 10am–2pm. €2. The Folk Art Museum is one of the most enjoyable in the city, even though let down somewhat by poor lighting and labelling. Its five floors are devoted to collections of weaving, pottery, regional costumes and embroidery, along with other traditional Greek arts and crafts. On the mezzanine floor, the carnival tradition of northern Greece and the all-but-vanished shadow-puppet theatre are featured. The second floor features exhibits of gold and silver jewellery and weaponry, much of it from the era of the War of Independence. The highlight, though, is on the first floor: the reconstructed room from a house on the island of Lesvós with a series of wonderful murals by the primitive artist Theofilos (1868–1934), naïve scenes from Greek folklore and history, especially the independence struggle.

▼ SHOPS ON ADHRIANOÚ

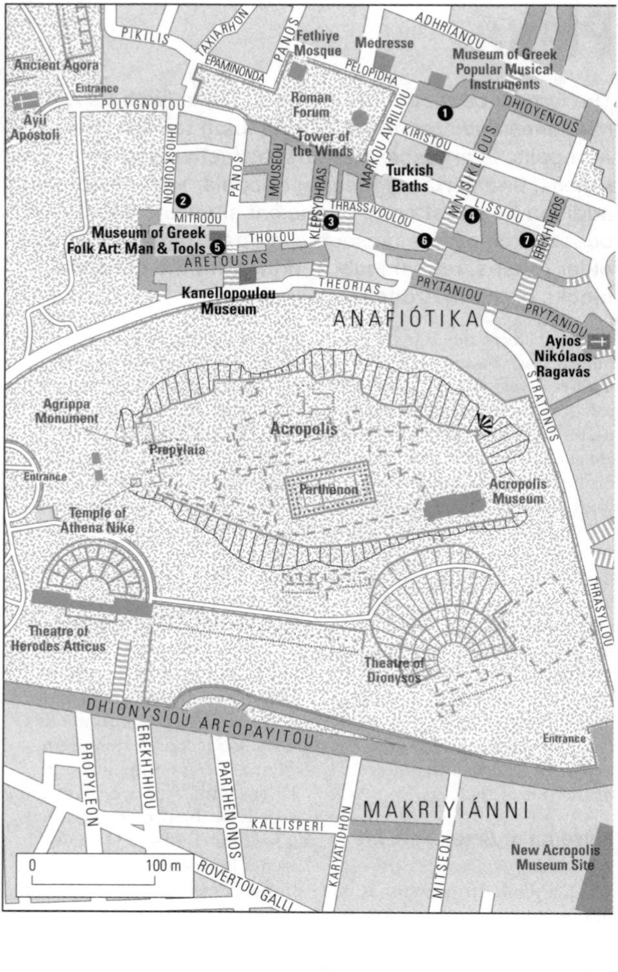

Children's Museum

Kydhathinéon 14. Tues–Fri 10am–2pm, Sat & Sun 10am–3pm. Free. Aimed at the under-12s, the Children's Museum is as much a play area as a museum. Labelling is entirely in Greek, and the place is primarily geared to school groups, who take part in activities such as chocolate-making – but it should keep young kids amused for a while. Permanent exhibits include features on the Athens metro, how computers work, and the human body.

Frissiras Museum

Monís Asteríou 3 and 7 ⓦwww.frissirasmuseum.com. Wed–Thurs 11am–7pm, Fri–Sun 11am–5pm. €6. Housed in two beautifully renovated Neoclassical buildings, the Frissiras Museum is

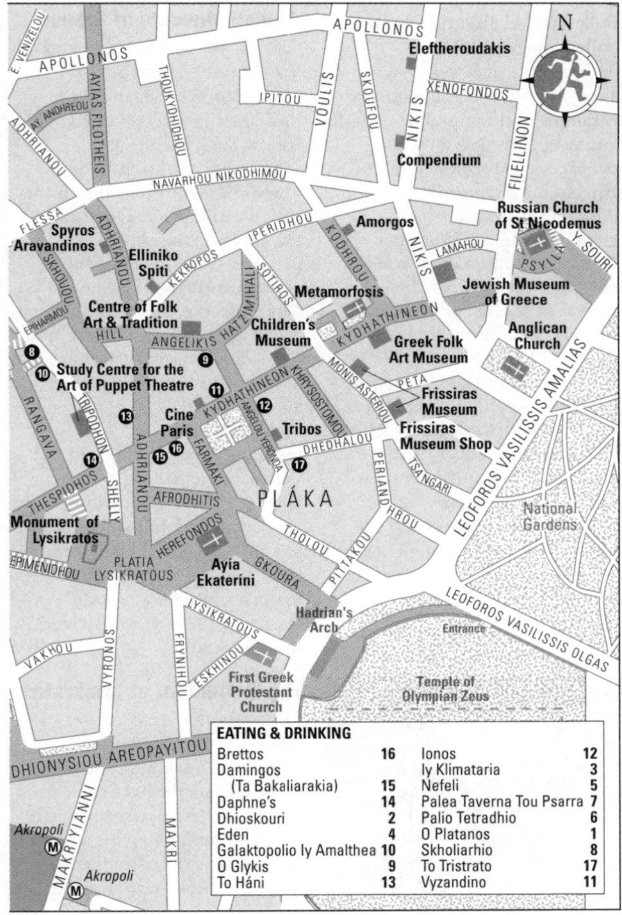

EATING & DRINKING

Brettos	16	Ionos	12
Damingos (Ta Bakaliarakia)	15	Iy Klimataria	3
		Nefeli	5
Daphne's	14	Palea Taverna Tou Psarra	7
Dhioskouri	2	Palio Tetradhio	6
Eden	4	O Platanos	1
Galaktopolio Iy Amalthea	10	Skholiarhio	8
O Glykis	9	To Tristrato	17
To Háni	13	Vyzandino	11

billed as Greece's only museum of contemporary European art. It has over three thousand works – mostly figurative painting plus a few sculptures, a regular programme of exhibitions, a fine shop and an elegant café. The space at no. 7 houses the permanent exhibition, which includes plenty of names familiar to English-speakers – David Hockney, Peter Blake, Paula Rego among them – as well as many less obvious Greek and other European artists. Temporary exhibitions, along with the shop and café, are at no. 3 a block away.

Centre of Folk Art and Tradition

Angelikís Hatzimiháli 6. Tues–Fri 9am–1pm & 5–9pm, Sat & Sun 9am–1pm. Free. The Centre of

Folk Art and Tradition houses a collection of costumes, embroidery, lace and weaving, along with musical instruments, ceramics, and icons and religious artefacts. Appropriately, it occupies the former home of Angelikís Hatzimiháli, a famous ethnographer whose championing of traditional Greek arts and crafts was one of the chief catalysts for their revival in the early twentieth century. The house itself – designed for her in the 1920s – is a large part of the attraction, with its cool, high rooms and finely carved wooden doors, windows and staircase. At the back, narrow stairs descend to the kitchen with its original range, while upstairs there's a library and rooms where classes are held to pass on the traditions of crafts like embroidery and weaving.

▼ MONUMENT OF LYSIKRATOS

Jewish Museum of Greece

Níkis 39. ⓦwww.jewishmuseum.gr. Mon–Fri 9am–2.30pm, Sun 10am–2pm. €3. Elegantly presented in a series of dimly lit rooms, with plenty of explanation in English, the Jewish Museum tells the history of Jews in Greece. Downstairs are art and religious paraphernalia, many of the pieces centuries old. The centrepiece is the reconstructed synagogue of Pátra, dating from the 1920s, whose furnishings have been moved here *en bloc* and remounted.

Upstairs, more recent history includes World War II and the German occupation, when Greece's Jewish population was reduced from almost 80,000 to less than 10,000. There are features, too, on the part played by Jews in the Greek resistance, and stories of those who survived the Holocaust.

The Monument of Lysikratos

In the southeastern corner of Pláka, the Monument of Lysikratos, a tall and graceful stone and marble structure from 335 BC, rises from a small, triangular open area with a couple of quiet tavernas. It's near the end of Odhós Tripódhon, a relic of the ancient Street of the Tripods, where winners of drama competitions erected monuments to dedicate their trophies (in the form of tripod cauldrons) to Dionysos. The Monument of Lysikratos is the only survivor of these triumphal memorials. A four-metre-high stone base supports six Corinthian columns rising up to a marble dome on which, in a flourish of acanthus-leaf carvings, the winning tripod was placed. The inscription tells us that "Lysikratos of Kikyna, son

▼ KANELLOPOULOU MUSEUM

of Lysitheides, was *choregos* (sponsor); the tribe of Akamantis won the victory with a chorus of boys; Theon played the flute; Lysiades of Athens trained the chorus; Evainetos was archon".

In the seventeenth century the monument became part of a Capuchin convent, which provided regular lodgings for European travellers – Byron is said to have written part of *Childe Harold* here, and the street beyond, Výronos, is named after him. The old Street of the Tripods would have continued in this direction – many important ancient Athenian buildings are thought to lie undiscovered in the vicinity.

Ayía Ekateríni Church

Platía Ayía Ekateríni. May–Oct Mon–Fri 7.30am–12.30pm & 5–6.30pm, Sat & Sun 5–10pm; Nov–April 7.30am–12.30pm, Sat & Sun 5–10pm. Free. St Catherine's Church is one of the few in Pláka that's routinely open. At its heart is an eleventh-century Byzantine original – although it has been pretty well hidden by later additions. You can see it most clearly from the back of the church, while in the courtyard in front are foundations of a Roman building. Inside, the over-restored frescoes look brand new, and there are plenty of glittering icons.

Kanellopoulou Museum

Theorías 12, cnr Panós. Tues–Sun 8.30am–3pm. €2. Though there's nothing here that you won't see examples of in the bigger muse-

The Anafiótika

The main arteries of Pláka, above all **Kydhathinéon** with its crowds of restaurants and **Adhrianoú**, home of the Manchester United beach towel and "Sex in Ancient Greece" playing cards, can become depressingly touristy. For a break, climb up into the jumble of streets and alleys that cling to the lower slopes of the Acropolis. There are still taverna tables set out wherever a bit of flat ground can be found up here, but there are also plenty of quieter corners redolent of a different era.

The whitewashed cubist houses of **Anafiótika**, as this quarter is known, proclaim a cheerfully architect-free zone. Many of the haphazard buildings were originally erected by workers from the island of Anáfi in the southern Aegean, who were employed in the mid-nineteenth-century construction of Athens. Unable to afford land, they took advantage of a customary law to the effect that if a roof and four walls could be thrown up overnight, the premises were yours at sunrise.

ums, the Kanellopoulou collection, exhibited in the topmost house under the Acropolis, is well worth a visit. On the lower floors the many gorgeous gilded icons first grab your attention, but there's also Byzantine jewellery, bronze oil lamps and crosses, and Roman funerary ornaments; some of the smaller items are exquisite.

Upstairs is ancient pottery and bronze, including items from Minoan Crete and from Egypt, and Stone Age tools. The top floor is perhaps the best of all, with pottery and gold jewellery from the Geometric, Classical, Hellenistic and Roman periods. Items here range from some astonishingly well-preserved large water jars and *kraters* to the bronze ram from the prow of a battleship, shaped like a dog's snout.

Museum of Greek Folk Art: Man and Tools

Panós 22. Tues–Sat 9am–2pm. €2. A brand-new branch of the Greek Folk Art museum, in another fine mansion, this is devoted to the world of work. The exhibits of tools and antiquated machinery concentrate on the pre-industrial world, with collections of agricultural implements and the like.

Turkish Baths

Kirístou 8. Wed & Sun 10am–2pm. Free. Constructed originally in the 1450s, though with many later additions, the Turkish Baths were in use right up to 1965. Newly restored, they offer an insight into a part of Athens' past that is rarely glimpsed and are well worth a look. Traditionally, the baths would have been used in shifts by men and women, although expansion in the nineteenth century provided the separate facilities you see today. The *tepidarium* and *caldarium*, fitted out in marble with domed roofs and rooflights, are particularly beautiful. The underfloor and wall heating systems have been exposed in places, while upstairs there are photos and pictures of old Athens. Labelling throughout is in Greek only, so it may be worth using the audio tour on offer (€1, plus a deposit).

Shops

Amorgos

Kódhrou 3. A small handicraft shop filled with tasteful woodcarvings, needlework, lamps, lace and shadow puppets.

Cine Paris

Kydhathinéon 22. Cult movies shown on the rooftop, while at

▼ OLD HOUSES AGAINST ACROPOLIS WALLS

▲ PLÁKA ALLEYWAY

street level there's a small shop where you can pick up that poster of *Gone With the Wind* in Greek you always hankered after.

Compendium

Níkis 28. Long-established, friendly and good-value English-language bookshop, with a small secondhand section; it also sells magazines.

Eleftheroudakis

Níkis 20. Not as impressive as the main branch of this bookshop chain (see p.92), Eleftheroudakis still has a good selection of English-language books, maps and guides.

Elliniko Spiti

Kekropós 14, just off Adhrianoú. Amazing artworks and pieces of furniture from found materials, including driftwood metal and marble. Probably too big to take home (for your wallet as well as your suitcase), but well worth a look.

Frissiras Museum Shop

Monís Asteríou 3. Classy store in this modern art museum selling posters, cards and upmarket gifts.

Spyros Aravandinos

Adhrianoú 114. Perhaps the ultimate tourist shop. With a branch directly opposite at no. 95, between them they sell every souvenir conceivable, from shadow puppets, sponges and shells to tacky T-shirts and priapic Pans.

Tribos

Angélou Yéronda 9. Alternative gift shop that's more interesting than most, with folk art and puppets among the hippy accoutrements.

Bars

Brettos

Kydhathinéon 41 ☎210 32 32 110. By day a liquor store, selling mainly the products of their own family distillery, at night *Brettos* is one of the few bars in Pláka. It's a simple, unpretentious place with barrels along one wall and a huge range of bottles, backlit at night, along another.

Cafés

Dhioskouri

Dhioskoúron, cnr Mitröon. Popular café right on the edge of Pláka overlooking the Agora. Simple food – salads and omelettes – as well as the inevitable frappés and cappuccinos.

Galaktopolio Iy Amalthea

Tripódhon 16. Tasteful if pricey "dairy", serving mostly crêpes as well as non-alcoholic drinks.

O Glykis

Angélou Yéronda 2. A secluded corner under shaded trees just off busy Kydhathinéon, frequented by a young Greek crowd. It has a mouthwatering array of sweets, as well as cold and hot appetizer plates.

Ionos

Angélou Yéronda 7. Good coffees and snacks, but above all a great place to people-watch on the busy Platía Filomoússou Eterías.

To Tristrato

Dhedhálou 34, cnr Angélou Yéronda. Daily 2pm–midnight. Coffee, fruit juices, salads, eggs, desserts and cakes. Exquisitely decorated but expensive.

Restaurants

Damingos (Ta Bakaliarakia)

Kydhathinéon 41 ⓣ210 32 25 084. Eves only; closed mid-July to end Aug. Tucked away in a basement since 1865, this place has dour service, but the old-fashioned style (hefty barrels in the back room filled with the family's home vintages including a memorable retsina, excellent cod with garlic sauce and good value make up for it.

▼ TAVERNA TABLES

Daphne's

Lissikrátous 4 ⓣ210 32 27 971, ⓦwww.daphnesrestaurant.gr. If you want to impress the in-laws, this is the place to bring them. Everyone from the Clintons through half of Europe's royalty to Angelina Jolie has eaten here – and they make sure you know it. Classy Greek food is served in an attractive courtyard out back – expect to spend at least €50 a head.

Eden

Lissíou 12, off Mnisikléous ⓣ210 32 48 858. Closed Tues. The city's oldest and classiest vegetarian restaurant, in a retro setting on the ground floor of an old mansion. Dishes include mushroom pie, chilli and soya lasagne; portions aren't huge but are very tasty.

To Háni

Adhrianoú 138 ⓣ210 32 28 966. Right in the heart of pedestrianized Adhrianoú, this slightly old-fashioned place has linen tablecloths and tables in a garden courtyard at the rear as well as on the street in front. Prices are high for standard Greek food, justified by the position and because they often have good traditional music.

Iy Klimataria

Klepsýdhras 5 ⓣ210 32 11 215. Eves only. Having recently celebrated its centenary, this unpretentious and pleasant taverna has decent inexpensive food, mainly grilled meat and fish. In winter, you're likely to be treated to live guitar and accordion music, which inspires sing-alongs by

▲ TAVERNA CLOSE-UP

the mostly Greek clientele. In the summer, the roof opens.

Nefeli

Pános 24, cnr Aretoúsas ☎210 32 12 475. Taverna eves only, Ouzerí open all day. Delightful setting, with tables under a secluded grape arbour or in an old mansion with a panoramic view, on a peaceful side street. Does a small but interesting selection of moderately priced classic Greek dishes such as veal and lamb *stamna* (casserole baked in a clay pot). There's live Greek music most nights and a small dance floor. The adjacent synonymous *ouzerí*, overlooking the church of Ayía Anna, is a busier local hangout favoured by young Greeks.

Palea Taverna Tou Psarra

Erekhthéos 16 at Erotókritou ☎210 32 18 733. A restored old mansion in a splendid setting, on a tree-shaded and bougainvillea-draped pedestrian crossroads. You're best off sticking to the *mezédhes*, which include humble standards as well as pricier seafood and fish dishes.

Palio Tetradhio

Mnisikléous 26, cnr Thrassívoulou ☎210 32 11 903. One of the tavernas with tables set out on the stepped streets beneath the Acropolis. The food is a cut above that of most of its neighbours, though you pay for the romantic setting.

O Platanos

Dhioyénous 4 ☎210 32 20 666. One of the oldest tavernas in Pláka, with outdoor summer seating under the namesake plane tree around the corner from the Roman agora. Reasonably-priced specialities include chops and roast lamb with artichokes or spinach and potatoes. The barrelled retsina is the real thing.

Skholiarhio

Tripódhon 14 ☎210 32 47 605. Attractive, split-level taverna, also known as *Ouzerí Kouklis*, with a perennially popular summer terrace, screened from the street. It has a great selection of *mezédhes* (€2–4 each), brought out on long trays so that you can point to the ones that you fancy. Especially good are the flaming sausages, *bouréki* (thin pastry filled with ham and cheese) and grilled aubergine, and the house red wine is palatable and cheap.

Vyzandino

Kydhathinéon 18, on Platía Filomoússou Eterías ☎210 32 27 368. Reliable, traditional taverna that still attracts locals on this busy, touristy square. Take a look in the kitchen at the moderately priced daily specials, such as stuffed tomatoes, *youvétsi* and the like.

Monastiráki and Psyrrí

Monastiráki and Psyrrí are enjoyable parts of Athens. Less touristy than Pláka to the south, there are nevertheless plenty of sights and extensive opportunities for eating, drinking and shopping. The Monastiráki area has been a commercial hub of the city since Roman times at least. The Roman Forum is still one of the major attractions here, and though the district is no longer at the heart of the city's business life, its streets are still crowded with shops and offices. The area around the Forum feels like an extension of Pláka, with its narrow lanes and traces of the ancient. To the east, though, Odhós Ermoú and parallel Mitropóleos are noisier, busier and more geared to everyday living.

The traffic-free upper half of Ermoú is one of the city's prime shopping streets: if you're after Zara or Marks & Spencer, Mothercare or Benetton, this is the place to head for. Funkier shops can be found in the Flea Market area around Platía Monastirakíou.

Between them, Monastiráki and Psyrrí probably have more eating places per square foot than anywhere else in Athens. Their characters are quite different, though. Monastiráki restaurants tend to be simple and functional – especially the line of places that spills onto Mitropóleos as it heads up from Platía Monastirakíou.

Psyrrí is more of a place for an evening out – home to a throng of trendy restaurants, *mezedhopolía* and bars. Buzzing till late every evening, it doesn't have a great deal to offer by day, although the cafés seem to attract crowds whatever the time. Psyrrí's own website – Ⓦwww.psirri.gr – is an excellent place to find out what's going on and lists virtually every restaurant, bar, shop and gallery in the area.

Roman Forum

Entrance at Pelopídha, cnr Eólou. Daily: April–Sept 8am–7pm; Oct–March 8.30am–3pm. €2 or joint Acropolis ticket. The Roman Forum was built during the reign of Julius Caesar and his successor Augustus as an extension of the older ancient Greek agora. Its main entrance was on the west side, through the Gate of Athena Archegetis, which, along with the Tower of the Winds (see opposite), is still the most prominent remain on the site.

▼ ROMAN FORUM

which have been excavated. Inside the fenced site, but just outside the market area to the east, are the foundations of public latrines dating from the first century AD.

This gate marked the end of a street leading up from the Greek agora, and its four surviving columns give a vivid impression of the grandeur of the original portal. On the side facing the Acropolis you can still make out an engraved edict of Hadrian announcing the rules and taxes on the sale of oil. On the opposite side of the Forum, a second gateway is also easily made out, and between the two is the marketplace itself, surrounded by colonnades and shops, some of

The Tower of the Winds

Roman Forum. The best preserved and easily the most intriguing of the ruins inside the Forum site is the graceful octagonal structure known as the Tower of the Winds. This predates the Forum, and stands just outside the main market area. Designed in the first century BC by Andronikos of Kyrrhos, a Syrian astronomer, it served as a compass, sundial, weather vane and water clock – the last powered by a stream from one of the Acropolis springs.

Roman Athens

In 146 BC the **Romans** ousted Athens' Macedonian rulers and incorporated the city into their vast new province of Achaia. The city's status as a renowned seat of learning and great artistic centre ensured that it was treated with respect, and Athenian artists and architects were much in demand in Rome. Not much changed, in fact: there were few major construction projects, and what building there was tended to follow classical Greek patterns.

The **history** of this period was shaped for the most part by the city's alliances, which often proved unfortunate. In 86 BC, for example, Sulla punished Athens for its allegiance to his rival Mithridates by burning its fortifications and looting its treasures. His successors were more lenient; Julius Caesar offered a free pardon after Athens had sided with Pompey, and Octavian (Augustus) showed similar clemency when Athens harboured Brutus following Caesar's assassination.

The one Roman emperor who did spend a significant amount of time in Athens, and left his mark here, was **Hadrian** (reigned 117–138 AD). Among his grandiose monuments are Hadrian's Arch, a magnificent and immense library and (though it had been begun centuries before) the Temple of Olympian Zeus. A generation later, **Herodes Atticus**, a Roman senator who owned extensive lands in Marathon, became the city's last major benefactor of ancient times.

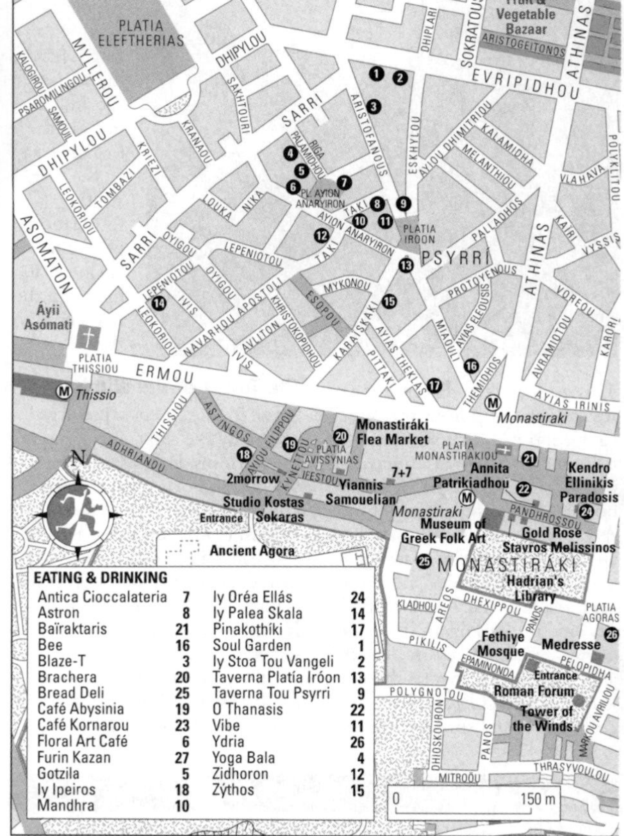

Each face of the tower is adorned with a relief of a figure floating through the air, personifying the eight winds. Beneath each of these it is still possible to make out the markings of eight sundials.

The semicircular tower attached to the south face was the reservoir from which water was channelled into a cylinder in the main tower; the time was read by the water level viewed through the open northwest door. On the top of the building was a bronze weather vane in the form of the sea god, Triton. In Ottoman times, dervishes used the tower as a *tekke* or ceremonial hall, terrifying their superstitious Orthodox neighbours with their chanting, music and whirling meditation.

Fethiye Tzami and the medresse

In the area around the Roman Forum can be seen some of the few visible reminders of the Ottoman city. The oldest mosque in Athens, the Fethiye Tzami, built in 1458, actually

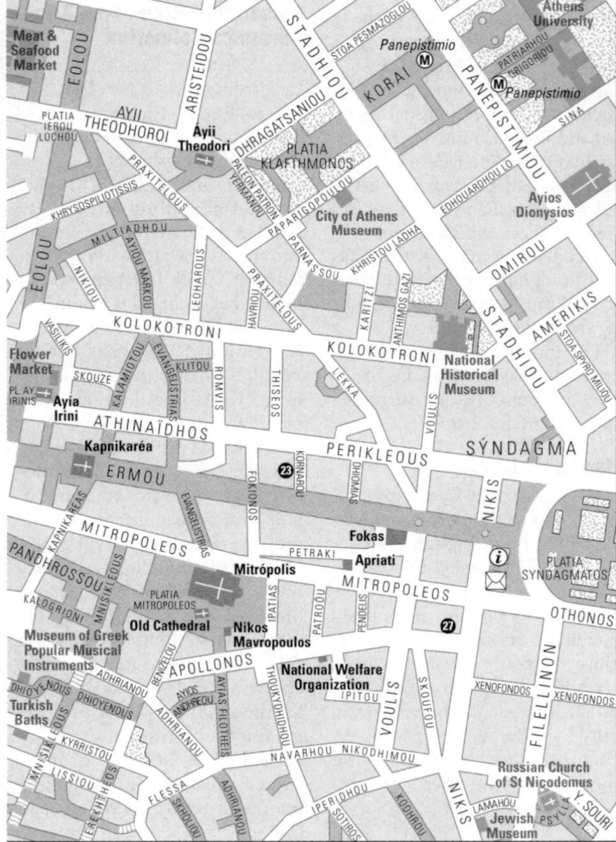

occupies a corner of the Forum site. It was dedicated by Sultan Mehmet II, who conquered Constantinople in 1453 (*fethiye* means "conquest" in Turkish). There's a fine, porticoed entrance, but sadly, you can't see inside, as it's now used as an archeological warehouse.

Across Eólou from here, more or less opposite the Forum entrance, the gateway and single dome of a **medresse**, an Islamic school, survive. During the last years of Ottoman rule and the early years of Greek independence, this was used as a prison and was notorious for its bad conditions; a plane tree in the courtyard was used for hangings. The prison was closed in the 1900s and most of the building torn down. Also nearby are the Turkish Baths (p.66).

Museum of Greek Popular Musical Instruments

Dhioyénous 1–3. Tues & Thurs–Sun 10am–2pm, Wed noon–6pm. Free.
Superbly displayed in the rooms of a Neoclassical building, the Museum of Greek Popular

Musical Instruments traces the history of virtually everything that has ever been played in Greece, including (in the basement) some more unusual festival and liturgical instruments such as triangles, livestock bells and coin garlands worn by carnival masquers. Reproductions of frescoes show the Byzantine antecedents of many instruments, and headphone sets are provided so you can hear the music made by the various exhibits.

The museum shop has an excellent selection of CDs for sale, concentrating, not surprisingly, on traditional Greek music.

Hadrian's Library

Áreos cnr Dhexíppou. Bordering the north end of the Forum site, and stretching right through from Áreos to Eólou, stand the surviving walls and columns of Hadrian's Library, an enormous building that once enclosed a cloistered court of a hundred columns. Though closed to the public, you get a good view from outside of the many surviving columns, as well as an idea of the sheer scale of the place.

▲ CERAMICS MUSEUM

Museum of Greek Folk Art: Ceramics Collection

Áreos 1. April–Sept Tues–Sun 8am–7pm; Oct–March Tues–Sun 8.30am–3pm. €2. Squeezed between the walls of Hadrian's library and the shacks of Pandhróssou stands the Mosque of Tzisdarákis. Built in 1759, it has had a chequered life – converted to a barracks and then a jail after Greek independence, before becoming the original home of the Greek Folk Art Museum in 1918. Today, as a branch of that museum, it houses the Kyriazópoulos collection of ceramics – the legacy of a Thessaloníki professor. Good as it is, the collection is in all honesty likely to excite you only if you have a particular interest in pottery; most people will probably find the building itself, the only one of Athens' old mosques whose interior can be seen, at least as big an attraction.

Though missing its minaret, and with a balcony added inside for the museum, plenty of original features remain. In the airy, domed space, look out for the striped *mihrab* (the niche indicating the direction of Mecca), a calligraphic inscription above the entrance recording the mosque's founder and date, and a series of niches used as extra *mihrabs* for occasions when worshippers could not fit into the main hall.

Monastiráki Flea Market

Platía Monastirakíou gets its name from the little monastery church (*monastiráki*) at its centre. Full of vendors selling nuts and lottery tickets, fruit stalls and kiosks, this area has been a marketplace since Turkish times and is still the heart of a bustling commercial neighbourhood.

In each direction you'll see signs proclaiming that you are

▼ FLEA MARKET

entering the famous Monastiráki Flea Market. These days this is a bit of a misnomer – there's plenty of shopping, but mostly of a very conventional nature. To the east, Odhós Pandhróssou is almost entirely geared to tourists. One of the most famous and quirkiest of the shops here is that of Stavros Melissinos, the "poet-sandalmaker of Athens" (see p.76).

West of Platía Monastiráki, the flea market has more of its old character, and among the tourist tat you'll find shops full of handmade musical instruments, or chess and *tavlí* boards, as well as places geared to locals selling bikes, skateboards or camping gear. An alley off **Iféstou** is jammed with record and CD shops, with a huge basement secondhand bookshop. Around **Platía Avyssinías** shops specialize in furniture and junky antiques: from here to Adhrianoú, the relics of the real flea market survive in hopeless jumble-sale rejects, touted by a cast of eccentrics (especially on Sundays). Odhós Adhrianoú is at its most appealing at this end, with a couple of interesting antique shops, and some shady cafés overlooking the metro lines, Agora and Acropolis.

The Kapnikaréa

Mon, Wed & Sat 8am–1pm; Tues, Thurs & Fri 8am–12.30pm & 5–7.30pm; Sun 8–11.30am. Free. The pretty Byzantine church of Kapnikaréa marks more or less the beginning of the upmarket shopping on Ermoú, looking tiny in these high-rise urban surroundings. Originally eleventh century, but with later additions, it has a lovely little dome and a gloomy interior in which you can just about make out the modern frescoes. The church is allegedly named after its founder, a tax collector (*kapnós* means smoke – in the Byzantine era a tax on houses was known as the smoke tax).

Platía Mitropóleos

A welcome spot of calm among the busy shopping streets surrounding it, Platía Mitropóleos – Cathedral Square – is home to two cathedrals. The modern Mitrópolis is a large, clumsy nineteenth-century edifice; the old cathedral alongside it is dwarfed by comparison, but infinitely more attractive. There is said to have been a church on this site since the very earliest days of Christianity in Athens. What you see now dates from the twelfth century, a beautiful little structure cobbled together from plain and carved blocks from earlier incarnations – some almost certainly from that original church.

▲ KAPNIKARÉA CHURCH

Shops

2morrow

Kynnétou 3. Vintage women's clothing store in the flea market that also sells its own designs.

7+7

Iféstou 7. A choice selection of old and new rock and Greek music on vinyl and CD. There are several other music places nearby in the flea market.

Apriati

Mitropóleos 9, cnr Pendelis. Athenians love their jewellery, and this designer store – sandwiched between old-fashioned jewellers – is typical of the innovative upmarket style of the city.

Fokas

Ermoú 11. Department store at the heart of the fashion shopping area.

Gold Rose

Pandhróssou 85. Interesting little shop with a wide range of jewellery and decorative items, from icons to body piercings and even samurai swords.

Kendro Ellinikis Paradosis

Mitropóleos 59 or Pandhróssou 36. This pleasant upstairs emporium opens to Mitropóleos on one side and Pandhróssou on the other. There's a wide selection of traditional arts and crafts, especially ceramics and woodcarving, and mercifully little of the hard sell often encountered in the nearby flea market. There's also a quiet café.

Museum of Greek Popular Musical Instruments

Dhioyénous 1–3. Excellent selection of CDs of traditional Greek music, albeit not cheap, plus some simple instruments to make your own.

National Welfare Organization

Ipatías 6, cnr Apóllonos. Rugs, embroideries, copperware – traditional craft products made in remote country districts.

Nikos Mavropoulos

Platía Mitropóleos 10. From the outside a glittering Aladdin's cave, this is one of a number of wonderfully old-fashioned stores behind the cathedral selling religious paraphernalia – icons, bible covers, robes, chandeliers and much more.

Stavros Melissinos

Pandhróssou 89. The "poet-sandalmaker" of Athens, Melissinos was something of a celebrity in the 1960s, hammering out sandals for the Beatles, Jackie Onassis and the like; it is said that John Lennon sought him out specifically for his poetic musings on wine and the sea, which Melissinos continues to sell alongside the

▲ CATHEDRAL SQUARE

footwear. The sandals translate better than the poems.

Annita Patrikiadhou

Pandhróssou 58. Genuine antiquities – pottery and coins mainly, some of them made into jewellery – are sold here, with official export licences to guarantee authenticity and legality. Prices are steep – but then many of the items are over 2000 years old.

Studio Kostas Sokaras

Adhrianoú 25. Overlooking the Stoa of Attalos, this place is packed with a wonderful jumble of antiques and curiosities, including old shadow puppets, brass doorknobs, musical instruments, pistols and more.

Yiannis Samouelian

Iféstou 36. Long-established musical instrument shop in the heart of the flea market, selling hand-made guitars, *lyra* and the like.

Cafés

Antica Cioccalateria

Platía Ayíon Anaryíron. It seems there's a café on every corner in Psyrrí, but if you fancy a change from frappé this place serves thirty types of chocolate drink as well as a similar variety of teas.

Bread Deli

Adhrianoú 52. Inside a glossy new shopping centre in the flea market district, this café/bakery offers a quiet retreat from the furore outside. Great cakes and other bakery treats, too.

Café Kornarou

Kornárou 4. A good place to break your shopping trip for coffee and a sandwich, just off the bustle of the main Ermoú shopping strip. Similar cafés can be found in many of the side streets north of Ermoú.

Floral Art Café

Platía Ayíon Anaryíron. Next door to the *Antica Cioccalateria*, the *Floral* has a summer roof terrace where you can escape the crowds.

Iy Oréa Ellás

Mitropóleos 59 or Pandhróssou 36. Tucked inside the *Kendro Ellinikis Paradosis* store, this atmospheric café has a small but inspired selection of traditional *mezédhes* at good prices. There's also a great view of the rooftops of Pláka on the slope towards the Acropolis.

Ydria

Adhrianoú 68 cnr Eólou. Platía Paliás Agorás, just round the corner from the Roman Forum, is packed with the tables of competing cafés. This is one of the best for a quiet coffee or breakfast; they also serve more substantial meals.

Restaurants

Baïraktaris

Mitropóleos 88, cnr Platía Monastirakíou. Over a century old, this lively restaurant occupies two buildings, the walls lined with wine barrels and photos of celebrities. Some tables are on the bustling pedestrian street, but for a cosier atmosphere eat inside with the local regulars, where there's often impromptu live Greek music. The straightforward, inexpensive menu includes *souvláki*, *gyros* and oven dishes such as *tsoutsoukakia* (meatballs in tomato sauce).

Brachera

Platía Avyssinías 3 ☎210 32 17 202. Eves (from 9pm) & Sun lunch only. Closed Mon. Upmarket, modern Greek and Mediterranean café/bar/restaurant in a restored mansion overlooking the flea market. In summer, the roof garden offers views of the Acropolis.

Café Abysinia

Kynnétou 7, Platía Avyssinías ☎210 32 17 047. Tues–Sun 10am–1am, Sat & Sun 10am–7pm. With dining on two floors, this restaurant is one of the best in Athens, popular with a local alternative crowd. The food, moderately priced, is also alternative – a modern take on traditional *mezédhes*. Live music most weekday evenings and weekend lunchtimes.

Furin Kazan

Apóllonos 2 ☎210 32 29 170. Closed Sun. Strikingly decorated and popular diner-style sushi bar in a central location.

Gotzila

Ríga Palamídhou 5 ☎210 32 21 086. Eves only. Sushi bar in this über trendy little street off Platía Ayíon Anaryíron. Mostly a late-night joint, and not badly priced.

Iy Ipeiros

Ayíou Filípou, just off Adhrianoú ☎210 32 45 572. Daytime only. Very basic, cheap taverna at the edge of Monastiráki flea market – popular with locals for lunch and handy for the Agora.

Mandhra

Ayíon Anaryíron 8, cnr Táki ☎210 32 13 765. Popular place right by the main square in Psyrrí, with live music most evenings and standard taverna fare at prices that reflect the location.

Iy Palea Skala

Lepeniótou 25, cnr Leokoríou ☎210 32 12 677. With seating inside an old house and on a terrace in summer, this place is generally packed and lots of fun. Excellent *mezédhes* and wine at reasonable prices to accompany the acoustic house band.

Iy Stoa tou Vangeli

Evripídhou 63 ☎210 32 51 513. Open Mon–Sat 6am–9pm (market hours); closed Aug. Congenial taverna with an authentic Greek atmosphere, frequented by local workers and liveliest during late lunchtime. The decor includes songbirds in a huge cage and a large butcher block in the corner where your meats are cut to order. It serves simple, inexpensive taverna appetizers, soups, grills and abundant Greek salads.

Taverna Platía Iróon

Platía Iróon 1 ☎210 32 11 915. With tables set out on the less crowded square in Psyrrí, this is a great place for people-watching; inside, there's often live music in the evening. The food includes excellent *fava* (hummus-like bean purée) and taverna standards, good value for the location.

Taverna tou Psyrri

Eskhýlou 12 ☎210 32 14 923. One of the most original and cheapest establishments in Psyrrí, offering tasty traditional fare, usually including fresh fish and some less well-known recipes. Menu in deliberately obscure Greek only, so it may be easier to choose from the kitchen.

O Thanasis

Mitropóleos 69. Reckoned to be the best *souvláki* and *gyros* place in this part of Athens, where there's plenty of competition. Inexpensive, and always packed with locals at lunchtime: there's no booking, so you'll have to fight for a table. Watch for the side dish of peppers, which are unusually fiery.

Yoga Bala

Ríga Palamídhou 5 ☎210 33 11 335. Eves only. A super-stylish, expensive Indian restaurant done out in gold and pink, catering to an upmarket Psyrrí crowd.

Zidhoron

Táki 10, cnr Ayíon Anaryíron ☎210 32 15 368. Closed Aug. A typical Psyrrí upscale *mezhedopolío*, painted bright yellow and in a great location right by the square. It serves tasty Middle Eastern foods like *pastourmás*, *haloúmi* and hummus, as well as Greek favourites such as baked feta, grilled peppers and baked aubergine.

Zýthos

Karaïskáki 28 ☎210 33 14 601. This "beer restaurant" lays more emphasis on the beer than the food – claiming to serve 120 beers plus eight from the barrel. The accompanying dishes have an appropriately Germanic influence.

Bars

Astron

Táki 3 ☎697 74 69 356. Eves only. One of Psyrrí's busiest bars – partly perhaps because it's so small – which gets really packed when the guest DJs crank it up later on.

Bee

Miaoúli 6 cnr Thémidos ☎210 32 12 624. Closed Sun. Thanks to a location right by an exit from Monastiráki metro station on the way up to Psyrrí, this cool, modern, moodily lit bar is a popular meeting place. Food is served during the day.

Soul Garden

Evripídhou 65 ☎210 33 10 907. Popular bar/restaurant with the emphasis on bar, serving Thai-influenced food, with a garden in summer, fine cocktails and a top-floor club (Fri & Sat).

Clubs

Blaze-T

Aristophánous 30 ☎210 32 34 823. Freestyle disco with sounds ranging from hip-hop to techno.

Vibe

Aristophánous 1 ☎210 32 47 94. Minimalist, Japanese-style decor and frequent "happenings" at this bar/club, featuring guest DJs playing everything from trance to house.

Live music

Pinakothíki

Ayías Théklas 5 ☎210 32 47 741. Closed Sun. Small, cosy folk music venue with appearances from respected Greek and foreign artists.

▲ CAFÉ IN PSYRRÍ

Thissío, Gázi and Áno Petrálona

West of the Acropolis rise three substantial hills: Filopáppou, Pnyx and the Hill of the Nymphs. Easily accessed from Dhionysíou Areopayítou or Apóstolou Pávlou, the pedestrianized streets that run around the Acropolis site, they offer famous views of the city, looking down over the Acropolis itself. There are also plenty of paths for not too strenuous walking.

On the far side of Filopáppou lies the quiet, residential neighbourhood of Áno Petrálona, among the least spoilt in Athens, and with some of the city's best tavernas.

Thissío, to the north of here, is an increasingly fashionable address where new bars and cafés are edging out the more traditional places.

The Kerameikos site, north again, is remarkably little visited considering the riches inside – above all, the remains of the main cemetery of ancient Athens.

Gázi, to the west and north of Kerameikos, is a former industrial area where the reinvention of the old gasworks as the Tekhnópolis cultural centre has sparked a rush of alternative bars and restaurants.

Between them, these places offer some excellent and authentic eating and drinking options – a welcome antidote to Plaka's tourist traps. You'll find everything from the lively, youth-oriented bars and restaurants of Gázi to positively sleepy, old-fashioned tavernas in Áno Petrálona. Thissío, easily accessed by metro, has a good mix, with some of the best night-time views of the Acropolis from cafés around the traffic-free junction of Apóstolou Pávlou and Iraklidhón. It also provides some lively nightlife, drawing a younger crowd. In Gázi, the trendy spots are more scattered, and the streets, some partly derelict, can feel threatening at night, so you may want to take

▼ DHIONYSÍOU AREOPAYÍTOU

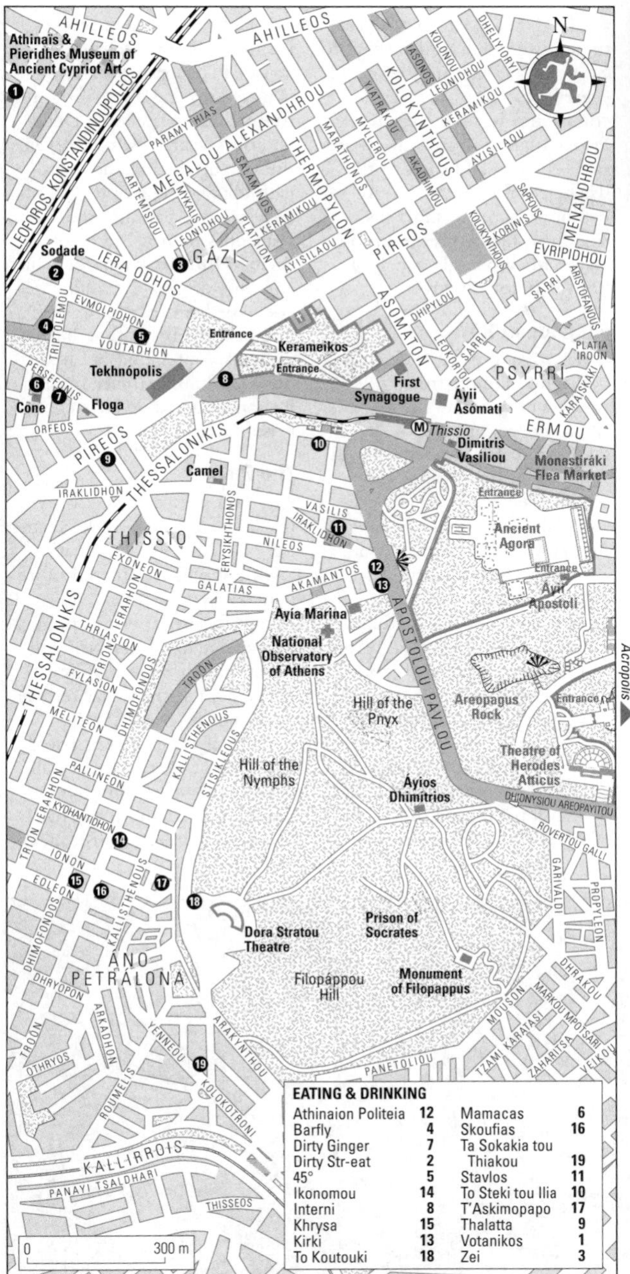

EATING & DRINKING

Athinaion Politeia	12	Mamacas	6
Barfly	4	Skoufias	16
Dirty Ginger	7	Ta Sokakia tou Thiakou	19
Dirty Str-eat	2	Stavlos	11
45°	5	To Steki tou Ilia	10
Ikonomou	14	T'Askimopapo	17
Interni	8	Thalatta	9
Khrysa	15	Votanikos	1
Kirki	13	Zei	3
To Koutouki	18		

a taxi. Gázi is a late-night place: there's not much point trying to eat before 9, or drink before 11 – preferably later. It really comes into its own late on Friday night and over the weekend – by day, and early in the week, it can be deserted. Áno Petrálona, too, is a short taxi ride from the centre, and most places are also easily accessible from Petrálona metro.

Filopáppou Hill

A network of paths leads from traffic-free Dhionysíou Areopayítou, below the Acropolis entrance, up Filopáppou Hill, also known in antiquity as the "Hill of the Muses" (*Lófos Mousón*). It provides fabulous views of the Acropolis and the city beyond, especially at sunset (although night-time muggings have occurred here, so take care).

This strategic height has played an important, if generally sorry, role in the city's history. In 1687 it was from here that the shell that destroyed the roof of the Parthenon was lobbed; more recently, the colonels placed tanks on the slopes during their coup of 1967. The hill's summit is capped by a grandiose monument to a Roman senator and consul, Filopappus, who is depicted driving his chariot on its frieze. To the west is the Dora Stratou Theatre (see p.169). On the way up the hill, the main path follows a line of truncated ancient walls, past the attractive sixteenth-century church of **Áyios Dhimítrios**, inside which are some original Byzantine frescoes. Further down, in the rockface near the base of the hill, you can make out a kind of cave dwelling, known (more from imagination than evidence) as the prison of Socrates.

The Pnyx

The Hill of the Pnyx was used in Classical Athens as the meeting place for the democratic assembly, which gathered more than forty times a year. All except the most serious political issues were aired here, the hill on the north side providing a convenient semicircular terrace from which to address the crowd. All male citizens could vote and, at least in theory, all could voice their opinions, though the assembly was harsh on inarticulate or foolish speak-

▼ VIEW FROM FILOPÁPPOU HILL

ers. There are some impressive remains of the original walls, which formed the theatre-like court, and of *stoas* where the assembly would have taken refreshment. This atmospheric setting provides commanding Acropolis views, while benches on the west side allow you to contemplate the vista across Pireás and out to sea.

Hill of the Nymphs

Observatory ⓦwww.noa.gr. Open first Fri of every month. The Hill of the Nymphs (Lófos Nymfón) is so called because nymphs were associated with the dusty whirlwinds to which this hill is particularly prone. Slightly lower and quieter than its better-known neighbours, it's a peaceful place with good views across to the western suburbs of Athens and beyond, as well as pleasant shaded walks. The summit is dominated by the impressive Neoclassical bulk of the National Observatory of Athens. First opened in 1842, though with many later additions, it has been in operation as a research institute ever since.

Kerameikos

Entrance on Ermoú. Entry included in joint Acropolis ticket. Providing a fascinating and quiet retreat from the Acropolis, the Kerameikos site encompasses, among other things, a section of the old city wall, two important gates to the city, the Pompeion, from which ceremonial processions started, and, above all, part of the principal cemetery of ancient Athens, which lay just beyond the walls. Always peaceful, there's something of an oasis feel about the place, with the lush Iridhanós channel, speckled with water lilies, flowing across it from east to west.

▲ OBSERVATORY

To the right of the entrance can be seen the double line of the **city wall**. The inner wall was hastily cobbled together by the men, women and children of Athens in 479 BC while Themistocles was pretending to negotiate a mutual disarmament treaty with Sparta. Two roads pierced the wall here: the great Dipylon Gate was the busiest in the ancient city, where the road from Pireás, Eleusis and the north entered; the Sacred Gate was a ceremonial entrance where the Ierá Odhós or Sacred Way entered the city – it was used for the Eleusinian and Panathenaic processions (see p.54 and p.137).

Between the two gates are the foundations of the **Pompeion**, a spacious building with a peristyle courtyard, used for the preparation of festival processions and where the sacral items used at the Panathenaic procession were stored. Branching off to the left from the Sacred Way, the Street of the Tombs, which is actually the old road to Pireás,

▲ KERAMEIKOS SITE

heads through the **cemetery**. The burial mounds that have been excavated along either side were reserved for the plots of wealthy Athenians. Some twenty can be seen, each containing numerous commemorative monuments, and their original stones or replicas reinstated. The flat, vertical stelae were the main funerary monuments of the Classical world; the sarcophagi that you see are later, from the Hellenistic or Roman periods. The sculpted crescent with the massive base to the left of the path is the Memorial of Dexileos, a 20-year-old warrior who died in battle in 394 BC; there's a relief scene of Dexileos on his horse. The adjacent plot contains the Monument of Dionysios of Kollytos, in the shape of a pillar stele supporting a bull. There are also many more humbler monuments, such as the poignant statue of a girl with a dog on the north side of the street.

Tekhnópolis

Pireós 100 ☎210 34 67 322, ⓦwww.athens-technopolis.gr. The former gasworks from which the Gázi district takes its name has been converted into a stunning series of spaces for concerts and changing exhibitions, mostly of contemporary art and photography. Two round gas-holders have become circular glass offices – one for Athens 98.4FM, the other for Tekhnópolis administration – while in the various pumping stations and boiler rooms surrounding them, galleries and exhibition halls of varying sizes, as well as a café, have been created, many with parts of the original machinery preserved. The only permanent display here is a small **Maria Callas Museum** (Mon–Fri 10am–5pm; free), whose collection of personal letters and photos, plus a pair of gloves and a fur coat, is really for fans only.

Athinaïs

Kastoriás 34–36 ☎210 34 80 000, ⓦwww.athinais.com.gr. A magnificent restoration of an early twentieth-century silk factory, the Athinaïs complex contains a theatre, music space, movie screen, two restaurants, a bar and café, exhibition halls, a museum and, the real purpose of the place, a sizeable conference centre. The **Pierídhes Museum of Ancient Cypriot Art** (daily 9.30am–1pm; €3) is beautifully presented in four small galleries, with some top-class exhibits including ceramics and very early glassware – although it might seem strange to be admiring these Cypriot objects in Athens. The museum shop is full of lavish (and lavishly priced) arty gifts, while upstairs are art galleries with temporary exhibitions. Details of what's on can be found on the website or in the local press.

Shops

Dimitris Vasiliou

Adhrianoú 1, Thissío ☎210 33 16 433. A neat little craft shop in Monastiraki's Flea Market. Items on sale include attractive and colourful ceramics and handmade jewellery from the Cyclades Islands.

Cafés

Athinaion Politeia

Apostólou Pávlou, cnr Akamántos. An enviable position in an old mansion, with great views from the terrace towards the Acropolis, makes this an excellent place to relax over a frappé. Light meals also served.

Kirki

Apostólou Pávlou 31 ☎210 34 69 960. Another café with a fabulous Acropolis view from its outdoor tables, serving good *mezédhes* as well as drinks and ice creams. Popular with the clientele of the late-night gay club (*Lizard*) upstairs.

Restaurants

Barfly

Voutádhon 34 ☎210 34 60 347. Eves only. One of the "neo-industrial"- style eating places popping up all around the Gázi area, *Barfly* is a moderate-to-expensive American-style diner with Mediterranean overtones. Good burgers with just a touch of Greece.

Dirty Ginger

Cnr Triptolémou 46 & Persefónis ☎210 34 23 809. Summer only: Mon–Fri eves only, Sat & Sun daytime & eves. A tasty mixture of Greek and foreign food at moderate prices, with garden seating in the summer. With lively recorded Greek music, it attracts a young crowd.

Dirty Str-eat

Triptolémou 12 ☎210 34 74 763. Eves only, closed Sun. This mid-range to expensive restaurant has now expanded its menu to include meat in addition to the wide selection of seafood – from sardines and smelt to thick fillets of sea bass and snapper.

Ikonomou

Cnr Tróön & Kydhantídhon ☎210 34 67 555. Basic, moderately priced home cooking served to packed pavement tables in summer. Recommended dishes are rabbit stew and oven-baked lamb.

Interni

Ermoú 152 ☎210 34 68 900. Eves only, closed Mon & Tues. Catering for a youngish clientele, *Interni*, with its minimalist decor, stresses Greek-European fusion food for serious diners and an easy "food bar" option for those with less time.

Khrysa

Dhimofóndos 81 ☎210 34 12 515. Eves only, closed June–Sept. Classy and fairly pricey restaurant with some pavement seating, serving international cuisine like smoked salmon and duck in various sauces, including curry.

To Koutouki

Lakíou 9 ☎210 34 53 655. Closed Sun. Like a country house with roof seating overlooking Filopáppou Hill, tucked just inside the flyover, this inexpensive, traditional taverna serves good mashed butter bean *fáva* and grilled meat.

Mamacas

Persefónis 41 ☎210 34 64 984. One of the restaurants that made Gázi fashionable, and still a favourite with the young, fashionable and well heeled. Traditional Greek food, *mezédhes*-style, with a modern twist. It's fairly pricey, and like everywhere here doesn't get lively till late – some time after midnight the DJs take over. Best to book.

Skoufias

Tróön 63 ☎210 34 12 210. Eves only, closed Sun. A pleasant and modern variation on the Greek taverna scene, with a variety of mid-range seasonal dishes – the honey-roast pork is the house speciality.

Ta Sokakia tou Thiakou

Stratigoú Kolokotróni 58 ☎210 92 49 614. A large, mid-priced taverna known for its pasta with lobster, lamb chops and mixed salads. Friendly management and service, with outdoor tables on a small square and live Greek music on weekends.

Stavlos

Iraklidhón 10 ☎210 34 67 206. Originally used as royal stables during the nineteenth century, now one of the more popular meeting points in the area, this hip hangout is as much an eating place as a bar, gallery and cafeteria. The food is a moderately priced mixture of fast fusion and standard Greek classics.

To Steki tou Ilia

Eptahálkou 5 ☎210 34 58 052. Closed Sun. This mid-range taverna on the pedestrianized road up towards Thissío station is so popular the owners have opened a namesake 200m further down. Renowned for some of the finest lamb chops in the city.

T'Askimopapo

Iónon 61 ☎210 34 63 282. Closed Oct–April. A wonderful winter taverna with unusual, reasonably priced dishes like meat in creamy sauces, and rooftop dining for balmy days.

Thalatta

Vítonos 5 ☎210 34 64 204. Closed Sun. Housed in a modernistic, marine-themed dining area, the fairly pricey *Thalatta* ("sea" in Ancient Greek) specializes in fish. Young in style and options, the menu is fresh, creative and busy.

Votanikos

Kastoriás 34–36 ☎210 34 80 000. A big, modern-brasserie style place in the Athinaïs complex, serving modern Greek food, as well as salads and the like. Mid-range to expensive.

Zei

Artemisíou 4, cnr Keramikoú ☎210 34 60 076. Eves and Sun lunch only; closed Mon & Tues. Charming old house serving imaginative Anatolian and Greek *mezédhes* in an enclosed courtyard. Best Thurs–Sat when it's busy and there's live rebétika and laïká music.

Bars

45°

Lákhou 18, cnr Voutadhon. A big, lively rock-music themed bar/café which makes a good place to meet up in Gázi.

Stavlos

Iraklidhón 10 ☎210 34 67 206. In the heart of the Thissío bar area, this daytime café/bar/restaurant evolves at night into a funky bar/club with jazz and soul sounds.

Clubs

Camel Club

Iraklidhón 74, Thissío ☎210 34 76 847. Opens 11.30pm. Indie rock and pop music are the themes at this newish bar club, drawing mainly a young crowd; Fridays feature music from the 1980s.

Cone

Triptolémou 35, Gázi ☎210 34 58 118. Daily midnight–4.30am. Small gay club that packs in the crowds with Greek music.

Floga

Perséfonis 19, Gázi ☎210 34 13 952. Daily 10pm–4am. Relaxed, upstairs gay bar/club with a view over the Tekhnópolis centre.

Raj Club

Plateía Ayíon Asomáton, Thissío ☎210 62 77 382. Opens midnight. Scattered over three levels, the *Raj* dishes out a mix of mainstream dance to a backdrop of ethnic, Japanese and 1970s decor motifs. Guest DJs make occasional appearances.

Sodade

Triptolémou 10, Gázi ☎210 34 68 657. Daily 11pm–3.30am. Stylish gay crowd and great music – one room plays Greek and mainstream, the other quality dance music.

Platía Omonías and around

While Pláka, Sýndagma and Kolonáki are resolutely geared to tourists and the Athenian well-heeled, Platía Omonías (Omónia Square) and its neighbouring streets revolve around everyday commerce and trade. Chaotic, gritty and working class, Omónia in fact couldn't be more different from ordered, chic and urbane Sýndagma.

It is, however, one of the liveliest areas of Athens and boasts an extensive patchwork of small shops and bazaars plying everything from power tools to flowers, punctuated with vast markets selling an abundance of fresh produce.

As far as more conventional sights go, the area is home to a clutch of small though quite enjoyable specialist museums and a series of elegant Neoclassical buildings strung out between Sýndagma and Omónia, a legacy of the ambitious building programme that followed Greece's independence in 1821.

The core of the city's modern market or bazaar is concentrated on Athinás and Eólou streets. The stores, though stocked mainly with imported manufactured goods, still reflect their origins in the Oriental *souk* system in the way that they are grouped together by specialization. Electrical goods, for example, dominate on Platía Klafthmónos and Aristídhou, while food stores cluster around the central market in the middle, especially along Evripídhou, and clothes are found on Eólou and Ayíou Márkou.

Barrelling resolutely southwards from Omónia Square towards the Acropolis, throbbing Odhós Athinás, once the area's red-light district par excellence and now home to a bustling series of markets and small shops, offers some of the most compelling sights, sounds and smells of urban Athens as East and West mingle in a riotous blend of cultures and peoples.

▲ OMÓNIA SQUARE

The meat and seafood market

Cnr Athinás and Evripídhou. The liveliest of the markets is the meat and seafood market, set in a grand nineteenth-century building. Its fretted iron awnings shelter forests of carcasses and mounds of hearts, livers and ears – no place for the squeamish. In the middle section of the hall is the fish market, with all manner of bounty from the sea glistening on marble slabs.

Platía Omonías and around

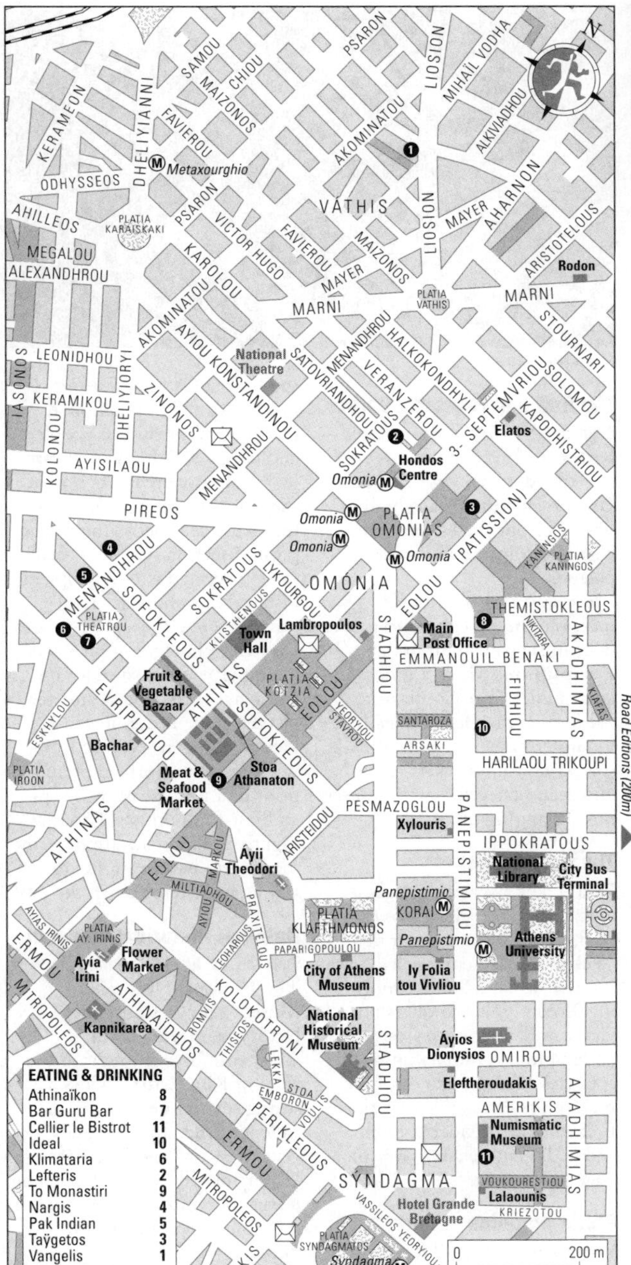

▲ SEAFOOD MARKET

The fruit and vegetable bazaar

Athinás. The fruit and vegetable bazaar is arrayed around a suspended archeological dig. Grocers pile their stalls high with sacks of pulses, salt cod, barrels of olives and wheels of cheese.

Just west of here, Athens' increasing multi-ethnicity is evident in the streets around **Evripídhou**, where a growing community from South Asia, predominantly Bengalis, gathers in large numbers around the spice-rich minimarkets and cheap and cheerful curry houses now springing up.

The flower market

Eólou. The flower market, gathered around the church of Ayía Iríni, has stalls throughout the week, but really comes alive with the crowds on a Sunday morning. Eólou itself also offers fine views: walk it north to south, coming from Omónia, and your approach takes you towards the rock of the Acropolis, with the Erechtheion's slender columns and pediment peeking over the edge of the crag.

Platía Omónias

Platía Omónias has little to offer in terms of aesthetics, but it is the heart of Athens for a good portion of the population. A continuous turmoil of people and cars, it is Athens at its earthiest and most urban. As one of the principal interchanges on the expanded metro, the underground section has been totally made over and is now stripped of the dingy shops it once housed, while the square above has been undergoing phases of seemingly perpetual renovations and makeovers. The perimeter of the square is dominated by kiosks selling everything from watchstraps to porn, clustered in front of a mish-mash of shops and fast-food outlets. Though slightly seedy in atmosphere, the square and its surrounds are as safe as anywhere else in the city.

National Historical Museum

Stadhíou 13. Tues–Sun 9am–2pm. €3. The National Historical Museum focuses on Greek history from the Fall of Constantinople through to the time of King Otto. There's a strong section on the War of Independence that includes Byron's sword and helmet. Unfortunately, minimal labelling leaves the visitor a little short of the historical context of the displays. There are also photographic archives, an ethnographic collection, a library and historical archives.

City of Athens Museum

Paparigopoúlou 5–7, Platía Klafthmónos ⓦwww.athenscitymuseum.gr. 10am–2pm, closed Tues. €5. The City of Athens Museum is concerned with a fairly narrow period of modern Greek history – the reign of King Otto and Athenian cultural life in the post-Otto period, and is housed in two of the oldest buildings in the city of Athens. The main building was the residence of the German-born King Otto in the 1830s before the new palace (now the Parliament, on Sýndagma) was completed in 1843. Appropriately enough, one floor is dedicated to the royal couple. Highlights include their exquisitely furnished private studies, dining room and throne room.

The second building is connected to the first via a covered walkway and comprises a collection of period furniture as well as an art gallery.

The museum's exhibits include paintings and prints, carvings and everyday items such as kitchenware, crockery and decorations, as well as rich collections of furniture displayed in a series of lavish period rooms which include the king's throne room as well as his personal office and that of his wife and consort Amalia. There is also a fascinating model of the city as it was in 1842, with just three hundred houses and a section of the ancient city walls.

Numismatic Museum

Panepistimíou 12. Tues–Sun 8.30am–3pm. €3. Housed in a grand building, this vast collection comprises over 600,000 coins, ranging from Mycenaean times through Classical, Macedonian and Roman to Byzantine and the modern era. In addition, there are weights, lead stamps, medals, precious stones and a rich archive of documents.

Shops

Bachar

Evripídhou 31. Aromatic bags of teas, herbs and medicinal remedies in large sacks.

▼ LITTLE INDIA

Eleftheroudhakis

Panepistimíou 17.The city's best bookshop, with five floors of English books. There's also an Internet café and an excellent cafeteria with a large selection of vegetarian dishes and sweets.

Iy Folia tou Vivliou (The Book Nest)

Panepistimíou 25, in the arcade and upstairs. The city's most eclectic selection of English-language fiction, with a good collection of recent academic work on Greece, and back issues of the *Korfes* hiking magazine. There's also a full-sized travel shop on the ground floor, with the complete line of Rough Guides and Anavasi maps.

Hondos Centre

Platía Omónias 4 ☎210 52 82 804. The city's top department store; though it's definitely no Harrods – low-ceilinged, cramped and crowded – the Hondos Centre is reasonably priced and stocks just about everything you could want. It has several floors of clothes, as well as a top-floor café with Acropolis views.

▲ PERIPTERO, OMÓNIA

Lalaounis

Panepistimíou 6. Home-base outlet of the world-renowned family of goldsmiths, whose designs are superbly imaginative and very expensive.

Lambropoulos

Eólou 99 ☎210 32 45 811. One of Athens' oldest and biggest department stores, Lambropoulos is also one of the biggest, stocking clothes, household goods, sporting goods and electrical items at reasonable prices.

Road Editions

Ippokrátous 39. Has a good mix of English and Greek travel guides, plus their own and other companies' maps.

Xylouris

Panepistimíou 39, in the arcade. Run by the widow of the late, great Cretan singer Nikos Xylouris, this is currently one of the best places for Greek popular, folk and (of course) Cretan music. Stocks items unavailable elsewhere.

Restaurants

Athinaïkon

Themistokléous 2 ☎210 38 38 485. Closed Sun. An old *ouzerí* that has recently relocated, but without losing its style – marble tables, old posters, etc. Good-sized, mid-priced *mezédhes* include shrimp croquettes and mussels simmered with cheese and peppers.

Bar Guru Bar

Platía Theátrou 10 ☎210 32 46 530. Busy and sometimes noisy "fun restaurant" with a Thai twist. The moderately priced dishes are pretty authentic, though dressed up to appeal to its fast, funky clientele.

Cellier le Bistrot

Panepistimíou 12 ☎210 36 38 525. With a Greek/international menu and a wide selection of wines, all dishes are carefully prepared and well presented. It's popular with the business community for lunch, while at night there's live piano music.

Ideal

Panepistimíou 46 ☎210 33 03 000. Closed Sun. A mid-range restaurant with bright, cheerful art deco decor, serving traditional, old-style *mayireftá*, imaginative daily specials and a decent selection of foreign-inspired dishes.

Klimataria

Platía Theátrou 2 ☎210 32 16 629. A mid-range, old-world type of taverna with rightly popular sessions of Smyrna-inspired rebétika music sessions. It serves a variety of rich *mezédhes*, with carafes of ouzo or draught retsina.

Lefteris

Satovriándhou 20 ☎210 52 25 676. A simple, cheap to mid-range grill restaurant serving decent *souvláki*, special stuffed beef patties and *mayireftá*; the draught wines are also very good.

To Monastiri

Central meat market (entrance from Eólou 81). Open 24hr. The best of the three restaurants here; the raw ingredients are certainly fresh, and it serves *patsás* (tripe and trotter soup), reputedly a good hangover cure.

Nargis

Sofokléous 60 ☎210 52 48 775. Tucked inside a *stoa*, this small Bengali canteen wins no prizes for decor, but has an authentic Indian atmosphere and meat and vegetarian curries at very low prices.

Pak Indian

Menándhrou 13 ☎210 32 19 412. A beautiful Indian restaurant, somewhat at odds with its surroundings. The food is excellent – fresh and delicately spiced, and there's interesting (recorded) music, as well as the occasional live concert.

Taÿgetos

Satovriándhou 4 ☎210 52 35 352. Closed Sun. A no-frills, budget restaurant with great *souvláki*, grilled lamb and chicken sold by the kilo. There's also a decent selection of *mayireftá* and palatable draught wine.

Vangelis

Sahíni 6, cnr Liossíon (sign in Greek). One of the friendliest and most authentic tavernas in central Athens, with a relaxing garden in use in summer. Mixture of grilled and oven food with superb *kondosoúvli* and *kokorétsi* their real speciality. Handy for the train station.

Live music

Elatos

Trítis Septemvríou 16 ⓣ210 52 34 262. Closed Wed. An eclectic assortment of *dhimotiká*.

Rodon

Márni 24, Platía Váthis, Ambelókipi ⓣ210 52 47 427. Closed in summer. The city's most important venue for foreign and Greek rock, soul and reggae groups – there's a good atmosphere in this converted cinema.

Stoa Athanaton

Sofokléous 19 ⓣ210 32 14 362. 3–6pm & midnight–6am; closed Sun & May–Aug. Rebétika place fronted by *bouzoúki* veterans Hondronakos and company, and serving good taverna food at reasonable prices, but drinks are expensive.

The Archeological Museum, Exárhia and Neápoli

Traditionally the stomping ground of anarchists, revolutionaries, artists and students, the area to the north of the main thoroughfares is nowadays home to a slightly more sedate, though still bohemian, crowd. The area's outstanding highlight is the fabulous National Archeological Museum, one of the world's top ten museums and an essential stop on any tour of Athens.

There are few specific sights otherwise, but it's a rewarding part of the city for a wander – restaurants, cafés and bookshops abound in the studenty area of Exárhia, while nearby Neápoli is home to a swathe of good, low-key tavernas, many featuring rebétika-style atmosphere and sometimes the music itself. Overlooking Neápoli, the little-visited Stréfis Hill (Lófos tou Stréfi) provides a welcome break from the densely packed streets and affords fine views of the city.

While not a tourist sight as such, the Neoclassical building housing the Polytechnic (Polytekhnío), the university's school of engineering and science, played a significant role in recent Greek history. In November 1973 students here launched a protest against the repressive regime of the colonels' junta, occupying the building and courtyards. In response, snipers fired indiscriminately into the protestors. Even today, nobody knows how many unarmed students were killed – estimates range from twenty to three hundred. The anniversary of the massacre is still commemorated by marches and sombre remembrance celebrations.

▼ EXÁRHIA SQUARE

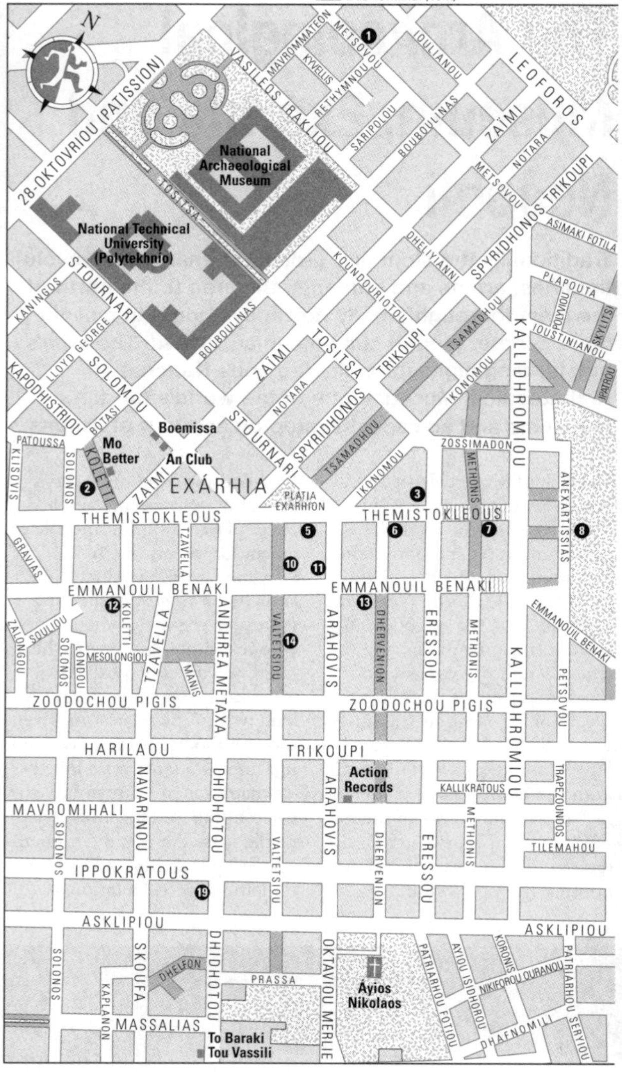

National Archeological Museum

Patissíon 44. €6. ⓦ www.culture.gr.

The National Archeological Museum is an unrivalled treasure house of Cycladic, Minoan, Mycenaean and Classical Greek art. The biggest attraction is Schliemann's gold finds from Grave Circle A at Mycenae, especially the funerary *Mask of Agamemnon*. The Mycenaeans' consummate art of intricate decoration is evident in a superb

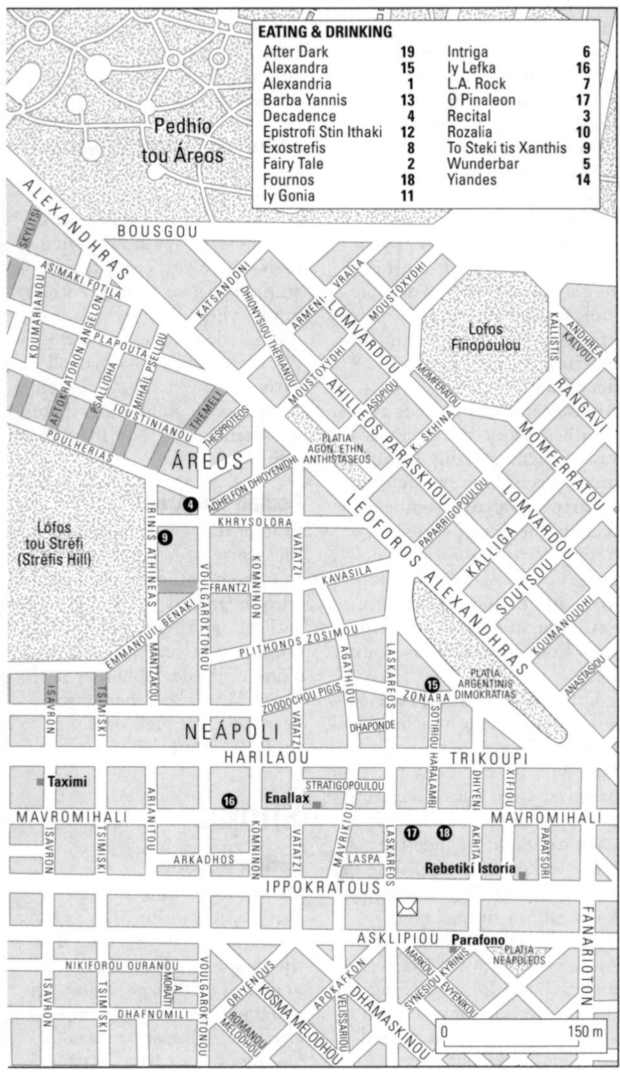

golden-horned *Bull's Head* and a miniature golden owl and frog from Nestor's palace at Pylos. Important finds from Tiryns include Cretan-style frescoes depicting chariot-borne women watching spotted hounds in pursuit of boar, and bull-vaulting reminiscent of Knossós, and a large mixing bowl (*krater*) with a chariot and warriors. Other delights are superb painted cups, with their scenes of wild bulls and long-tressed, narrow-waisted men, and an eye-catching cup decorated with twining octopuses and dolphins. Further references to Homer abound, most notably a magnificent *Boar's Tusk Helmet* and an ivory lyre with sphinxes adorning the soundboard.

The large collection of **Cycladic** art contains pre-Mycenaean pieces from the Aegean islands. Many of these idols suggest the abstract forms of modern Cubist art – most strikingly in the much-reproduced *Man Playing a Lyre*. Another unusual piece is a sixteenth-century-BC cylindrical vase depicting a ring of fishermen carrying fish by their tails.

Early sculpture highlights include the Aristion Stele of a Young Warrior, with delicately carved beard, hair and tunic-folds, and the Croesus kouros (statue of an idealized youth), both from the late sixth century BC.

The **Classical sculpture** collection includes a mid-fifth-century-BC bronze Statue of Poseidon, athletic body perfectly balanced as he stands poised to throw his trident. Other major Classical works include the Little Jockey of Artemission, the delicate bronze figure seeming too small for his galloping horse; the bronze Ephebe of Antikithira from the fourth century BC; and from the third century BC the bronze head of a philosopher, with furrowed brow and unkempt hair.

The most reproduced of all the later sculptures is a statue from the first century AD of a naked Aphrodite about to rap Pan's knuckles for getting too fresh. There is also an extraordinary bronze equestrian portrait statue of the Roman Emperor Augustus. Among other Roman pieces on display are various copies of the lost Pheidias Athena, the original centrepiece of the Parthenon.

Lófos tou Stréfi (Stréfis Hill)

Lying between the suburbs of Neápoli and Exárhia, this sudden break in the monotony of the cityscape is a little-visited oasis where you can escape for an hour or two from the street bustle. There is an easy path to the hill's low summit, where you can enjoy fine views over all parts of Athens. Take care here though with children, as there's an unfenced drop on the east side.

Pedhío tou Áreos

One of the few green areas in the centre of Athens, the Pedhío tou Áreos (Plain of Mars) is a fairly large park of trees, gardens and meandering paths. A long boulevard bisects the park, with a line of statues of heroes of the Greek War of Independence keeping silent vigil over the strolling visitors.

Shops

Action Records

Mavromiháli 51 ☎210 36 19 924. While you can find all the latest Greek and non-Greek CDs at the major retail stores on Stadhíou or Panepistimíou, this is the place to buy a genuine *bouzoúki*, *baglamás* or *laoúto* if you fancy your hand at playing Greek music.

Restaurants

Alexandra

Zonará 21 ☎210 64 20 874. Closed Sun. A converted old house with smart decor, verandah seating in summer and occasional accordion music. The imaginative, inexpensive dishes include aubergine croquettes, beetroot salad with walnuts, and meat in various sauces.

Alexandria

Metsóvou 13 ☎210 82 10 004. Closed Sun. Enjoy mid-range Egyptian and Mediterranean specialities in a restaurant setting reminiscent of Old Alexandria with palm plants, ceiling fans and a pleasant, shaded garden to dine.

Barba Yannis

Emmanouíl Benáki 94 ☎210 33 00 185. Very popular, mid-range restaurant, serving a varied menu of home-style oven food, with barrelled wine and a relaxed atmosphere. In summer you can dine al fresco on the pedestrianized street.

Epistrofi Stin Ithaki

Cnr Kolétti and Benáki. Closed Sun. Featuring Santoríni wine, this *ouzerí* does a good line in fish and seafood *mezédhes*.

Exostrefis

Lófos Stréfi. Entered from beside the basketball court on Stréfi Hill, this breezy *ouzerí* amidst the pines offers substantial portions of tasty food and a range of ouzo, as well as wine.

Iy Gonia

Arahóvis 59. Mushroom *saganáki*, meatballs, spicy sausages and octopus are among the delights at this *ouzerí*.

Iy Lefka

Mavromiháli 121 ☎210 36 14 038. Closed Sun. Moderate to mid-range old taverna with great butter bean purée *(fáva)*, black-eyed beans, baked and grilled meat with barrelled retsina. There's also summer seating in a huge garden enclosed by barrels.

O Pinaleon

Mavromiháli 152 ☎210 64 40 945. Closed Nov–April. A classic *ouzerí*-style establishment, serving rich *mezédhes* and meaty entrées, washed down with home-made wine. Advance booking is recommended.

▼ GROUNDS OF THE POLYTEKHNÍO

Rozalia

Valtetsíou 58 ☎210 33 02 933. Ever-popular mid-range *mezédhes*-plus-grill taverna, with excellent chicken and highly palatable barrelled wine. You order from the proffered tray as the waiters thread their way through the throng. In summer you can dine in the garden opposite.

To Steki tis Xanthis

Irínis Athinéas 5 ☎210 88 20 780. Closed Sun. A delightful old mansion with a roof garden that offers fine views across to Stréfis Hill. The mid-range house specialities include rabbit stew and *schnitzel*.

Yiandes

Valtetsíou 44 ☎210 33 01 369. A high-quality, moderate to expensive new restaurant serving a range of dishes, from cold cuts to stuffed mushrooms, as well as meat and fish recipes from Asia Minor.

Bars

After Dark

Dhiodótou 31 & Ippokrátous ☎210 36 06 460. Opens 9.30pm. A downtown youth hangout in happening Exárhia; the music runs from classic rock to present-day hits.

Fairy Tale

Kolétti 25 ☎210 33 01 763. Daily 10pm–3am. A classic city-style bar drawing an arty, largely lesbian crowd; guest DJs play a mixed Greek and non-Greek music selection. Also open Sunday afternoons for coffee and cake.

L.A. Rock

Themistokléous & Methónis 58 ☎210 38 44 024. Opens 9.30pm. A rock bar for all ages, encompassing musical tastes from the 1980s onwards, but especially mainstream guitar-based rock. The scene can be fast and furious.

Recital

Eressoú 64 & Themistokléous ☎210 38 05 556. Opens 7pm. One of the oldest rock bars in the Exárhia Square area. Pumped up rock blasts from the speakers to a crowd of mainly rock-savvy students and head-bangers.

Clubs

Decadence

Voulgaroktónou 69 & Poulherías ☎210 88 23 544. Opens 11pm. Popular with students, classic underground rock reverberates until late, while you can also catch some independent rock and electronic pop, and some live performances.

Fournos

Mavromiháli 168 ☎210 64 60 748. Opens 7.30pm. *Fournos* means "oven" in Greek – it can get

▼ O PINALEON

hot in this arty joint, where electronic pop and rock feature prominently. DJs and VJs complete the scene.

Intriga

Themistokléous & Dervenion 60 ⓣ210 33 00 936. Opens 11pm. Modern and classic rock echo through this Neoclassical building, as well as black and progressive rock, attracting students as well as serious barflies.

Wunderbar

Themistokléous 80, Platía Exarhíon. Opens 9am. Fans of electro and techno-pop gather at this alternative venue for non-mainstream sounds. The patrons tend to be neo-mods with eclectic dress and music sense.

Live music

An Club

Solomoú 13–15 ⓣ210 33 05 056. Entry from €6. Basement club featuring local and lesser-known foreign rock bands.

To Baraki Tou Vassili

Dhidhótou 3 ⓣ210 36 23 625. €13 entry includes first drink. Popular showcase for up-and-coming rebétika acts and other singer-songwriters.

Boemissa

Solomoú 19 ⓣ210 38 43 836. Midnight–late; closed Mon. Reservations recommended. Rebétika and regional folk music from all over Greece. Extremely popular with university students, who jam the dance floor and aisles. Drinks €6 (two drinks minimum).

Enallax

Mavromiháli 139 ⓣ210 64 37 416. Thurs–Sat. No cover charge, but reservation needed. Lively, friendly venue hosting various folk-style acts; drinks are €6. Live gigs mostly Thurs–Sat.

Mo Better

Kolétti 32. €6 entry includes drink. Cramped but fun bar on the first floor of a Neoclassical building, with hip-hop, punk and indie rock.

Parafono

Asklipíou 130A ⓣ210 64 46 512. Small, congenial place featuring Greek jazz bands.

Rebetikí Istoría

Ippokrátous 181, Neápoli ⓣ210 64 24 967. Closed Wed & July–Aug. Genuine rebétika sounds from a good company in a large old house; drinks cost €5.75, and tasty food is also served.

Taximi

Isávron 29 ⓣ210 36 39 919. Closed Sun & July–Aug. Crowded, long-established salon on the third floor of a Neoclassical building, attracting a crowd of all ages. Food is served, including fruit plates and mixed appetizers. There's no cover charge, but drinks cost €7.

Kolonáki & Lykavitós Hill

If you have money to spend, Kolonáki, a favourite haunt of expatriates, is the place to do it, catering as it does to every Western taste from fast food to high fashion. It's also from here that a funicular hauls you up to Lykavitós Hill, where some of the best views of the city are to be had. Close by are a couple of fine museums: one devoted to Cycladic Art; the other, the Benáki, an assembly of just about all things Greek, from Mycenaean artefacts to twentieth-century memorabilia. It was in this area that the fourth-century-BC foundations of Aristotle's Lyceum – where he taught for thirteen years and to which Socrates was a frequent visitor – were recently unearthed during excavation work for a new Museum of

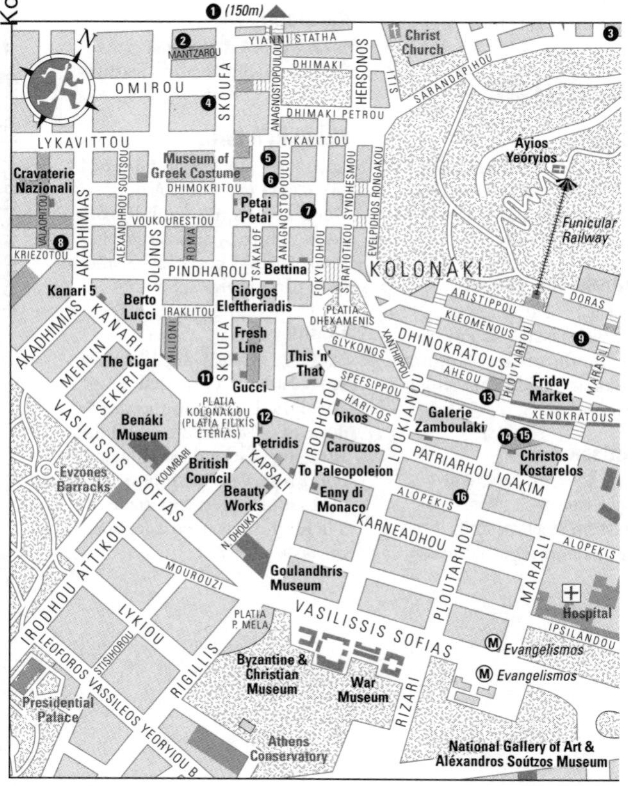

Modern Art, though these remain unvisitable. If you've the stamina, the other museums in the area – the War Museum, the Byzantine and Christian Museum, the National Art Gallery and the Aléxandros Soútzos Museum – may appeal but are mainly for enthusiasts. At night the area is at its livliest, with plenty of upmarket bars, cafés and restaurants. Further east, the more modern areas of Ilísia and Ambelókipi, have more good bars and music clubs, as well as the Mégaro Mousikís, Athens' princupal concert hall.

Kolonáki

Bordered by grand Neoclassical palaces at the bottom of Lykavitós and the residential areas higher up the hill, the centre of Kolonáki forms the city's chicest shopping district. Although not as architecturally inspiring as some of the more traditional neighbourhoods of Athens, it enjoys a superb site on the southwest-facing slopes

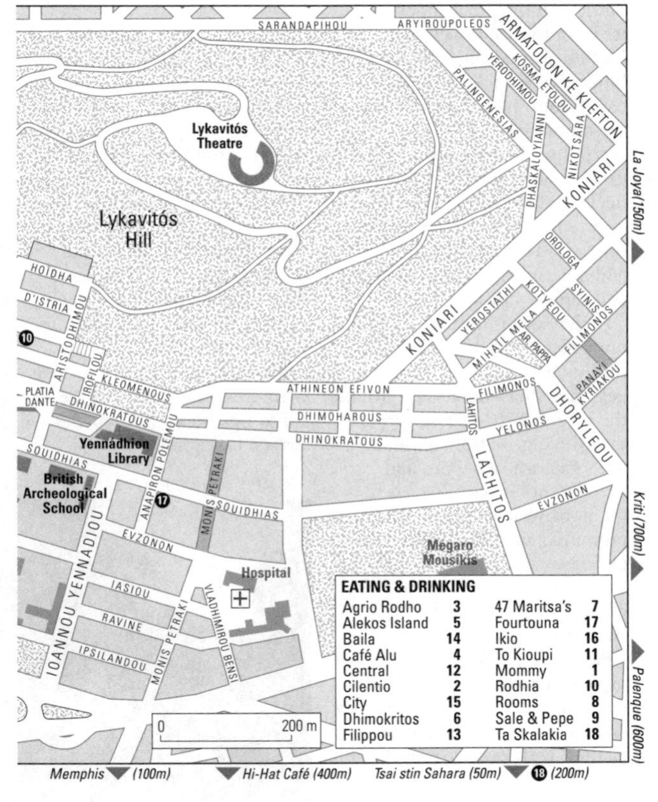

EATING & DRINKING			
Agrio Rodho	3	47 Maritsa's	7
Alekos Island	5	Fourtouna	17
Baila	14	Ikio	16
Café Alu	4	To Kioupi	11
Central	12	Mommy	1
Cilentio	2	Rodhia	10
City	15	Rooms	8
Dhimokritos	6	Sale & Pepe	9
Filippou	13	Ta Skalakia	18

▲ FUNICULAR

of Lykavitós, looking out over the Acropolis and National Gardens.

The heart of it all is officially called Platía Filikís Eterías but is always referred to as **Platía Kolonakíou**, after the ancient "little column" that hides in the trees on the southwest side. Dotted around the area are kiosks with stocks of foreign papers and magazines, and there are numerous cafés on Patriárhou Ioakím – stamping ground of Kolonáki's well-heeled residents – although the assorted cafés and pubs nearby on pedestrianized Tsakálof, Milióni and Valaorítou are better and slightly cheaper.

In the dozens of small, upmarket shops the accent is firmly on fashion and designer gear, and a half-hour stroll around the neighbourhood will garner the whole gamut of consumer style. Patriárhou Ioakím and Skoufá, with its cross-streets to the northwest, comprise the most promising area along with the pedestrianized Voukourestíou–Valaorítou–Kriezótou block, just below Akadhimías.

For more random strolling, the highest tiers of Kolonáki can be very enjoyable, with steep streets ending in long flights of steps, planted with oleander and jasmine.

Lykavitós Hill

Lykavitós Hill offers tremendous views at any time, but particularly from late afternoon onwards – on a clear day you can see the mountains of the Peloponnese. After dark, the shimmering lights of Athens stretch right across the Attica basin.

To get to the summit you can take a **funicular** from the top of Ploútarhou, not far from Kolonáki square (Mon–Wed & Fri–Sun 8.45am–12.40am, Thurs 10.30am–12.40am, every 10min in summer, otherwise every 30min; €4). For the more energetic, the principal path up the hill begins by the bus stop across from the *St George Lycabettus Hotel* above Platía Dhexamenís and winds through woods to the top. The lower part of the path is easy enough, running through shady pine trees; higher up, the going gets more exposed and strenuous, although you can take a break at a small café halfway, right opposite the Acropolis.

On the summit stands the small, whitewashed chapel of **Áyios Yeóryios** (St George), built in the nineteenth century. An expensive restaurant commands the adjacent terrace facing the Acropolis and the sea; it also operates a café on the terrace facing inland.

▼ KOLONÁKI STREET

▲ ÁYIOS YEÓRYIOS CHAPEL

The road up the hill goes to the open-air Lykavitós Theatre (see p.35). If you come down by the southeast slopes, you emerge near the lovely little enclave that the British and American archeological schools have created for themselves on Souidhías. Here, too, is the **Yennádhion Library** (Ⓣ210 72 10 536, Mon–Wed & Fri 9am–8pm, Sat 9am–2pm) with its large collection of books on Greece and an unpublicized drawer full of Edward Lear's watercolour sketches; good-quality and reasonably priced reproductions are on sale.

The Benáki Museum

Koumbári 1, cnr Vasilíssis Sofías Ⓦwww.benaki.gr. Mon, Wed, Fri & Sat 9am–5pm, Thurs 9am–midnight, Sun 9am–3pm. €6, temporary exhibitions €3. The often overlooked but fascinating Benáki Museum should not be missed. Housing a private collection donated to the state in the 1950s by Emmanouíl Benákis, a wealthy cotton merchant, exhibits range from Mycenaean jewellery, Greek costumes and folk artefacts to memorabilia from Byron and the Greek War of Independence, as well as jewellery from the Hélène Stathatos collection.

More than twenty thousand items are exhibited chronologically and clearly labelled; ancient finds are on the lower floors and the modern Greek artefacts on the upper floors. Among the more unusual items are collections of early Greek Gospels, liturgical vestments and church ornaments rescued by Greek refugees from Asia Minor in 1922. There are also dazzling embroideries and body ornaments, and some unique historical letters and photographs on the Cretan statesman Elefthérios Venizélos, Asia Minor and the Cretan Revolution.

The museum shop by the entrance stocks a fine selection of books on Greek folk art, CDs of regional music and some of the best posters and postcards in the city.

▼THE BENÁKI MUSEUM

Goulandhrís Museum of Cycladic and Ancient Greek Art

Neofýtou Dhouká 4 Ⓦwww.cycladic-m.gr. Mon, Wed, Thurs & Fri 10am–4pm, Sat 10am–3pm. €3.50. The small, private Goulandhrís Museum of Cycladic and Ancient Greek Art is an extremely well presented collection that includes objects from the Cycladic civilization (third millennium BC), pre-Minoan Bronze Age (second millennium BC) and the period from the fall of Mycenae to around 700 BC, plus a selection of Archaic, Classical and Hellenistic pottery; in fact, you may learn far more about these periods than from the corresponding sections of the National Archeological Museum.

From the **Cycladic period** are distinctive marble bowls and folded-arm figurines (mostly female) with sloping wedge heads whose style was influential on twentieth-century artists such as Moore and Picasso. Their exact purpose is unknown but, given their frequent discovery in grave-barrows, it's possible that they were spirit-world guides for the deceased, substitutes for the sacrifice of servants and attendants, or representations of the Earth Goddess.

Much of the top floor is devoted to a collection of painted **Classical** bowls, often showing two unrelated scenes on opposite sides – for example, the star exhibit depicts revellers on one face and three men in cloaks conversing on the other. Many of the more exquisite items date from the fifth century BC, the "golden age" of Classical Athens.

To round off the experience, there's a good shop, snack bar

▲ CYCLADIC MUSEUM

and shaded courtyard, from which a covered passageway leads to the nineteenth-century **Stathatos House**, magnificently restored as an extension for temporary exhibitions.

Byzantine and Christian Museum

Vasilíssis Sofías 22. Tues–Sun 8.30am–3pm. €4. Perhaps the best feature of the Byzantine and Christian Museum is its setting: a peaceful villa with courtyard that once belonged to the Duchesse de Plaisance, an extravagantly eccentric French philhellene and widow of a Napoleonic general who helped fund the War of Independence. To enjoy the exhibits – almost exclusively icons, housed in two restored side galleries – requires some prior interest. Labelling is sometimes Greek-only, and you are told little of the development of styles, which towards the sixteenth century show an increasing post-Renaissance Italian influence, owing to the presence of the Venetians in Greece.

War Museum

Cnr Vasilíssis Sofias & Rizári 2. Tues–Sat 9am–2pm, Sun 9.30am–2pm. Free. The only "cultural" endowment of the 1967–74 junta, the War Museum becomes predictably militaristic and right-wing as it approaches modern events such as the Asia Minor campaign, the civil war and Greek forces in Korea. Earlier times, however, are covered with a more scholarly concern, showing the changes in warfare from Mycenae through to the Byzantines and Turks. Among an array of models is a fascinating series on the acropolises and fortresses of Greece, both Classical and medieval.

National Art Gallery and Aléxandros Soútzos Museum

Vasiléos Konstandínou 50. Mon & Wed 9am–3pm & 6–9pm, Thurs–Sat 9am–3pm, Sun 10am–2pm. €6. The state's core collection of Greek art, from the sixteenth century to the present day, is combined in the National Art Gallery with the private collection of the Athenian lawyer Aléxandros Soútzos. Today, the whole shebang holds around 9500 paintings, sculptures and engravings as well as miniatures and furniture.

Although a slightly disappointing experience, it's worth checking out the work of Nikos Hatzikyriákos-Ghíkas (Ghika), a modern painter well represented on the ground floor, as well as the small group of canvases on the mezzanine by the primitive artist Theofilos, more of whose work can be seen at the Museum of Greek Folk Art in Pláka (see p.61).

A recent refurbishment has created a much more prominent area for temporary exhibitions, most of them major loans from the world's best museums, and these are definitely worth catching.

Shops

Beauty Works

Kapsáli & Neofýtou Doúka, Kolonáki ☎210 72 25 511. Favoured by Madonna and other celebrities, the Beauty Works cosmetics chain stocks all the classic brands.

Berto Lucci

Sólonos 8 ☎210 36 03 775. Well-priced men's and women's clothes and accessories at one of a chain of stores around Athens. Shoes and classy leatherwear feature also, including men's attaché cases.

Bettina

Pindárou 41 ☎210 32 38 759. Reliable, chic and classy clothes store – Greek designers such as Angelos Frentzos and Sofia Kokosalaki feature heavily.

▼ SHOPPING IN KOLONÁKI

Carouzos

Patriárhou Ioakím 14 ☎210 72 45 873. Part of a chain of upmarket boutiques selling high-quality clothing, with a great range of classic and formal clothes for both men and women, good-quality shoes and accessories.

Christos Kostarelos

Cháritos 44 ☎210 72 28 261. One of the most talented designers in Athens, Christos Kostarelos gives a new edge to native Greek design – the superb fluffy shawls are a good buy.

The Cigar

Kánari 21 ☎210 36 03 725. Fine cigars from Havana, Honduras and Nicaragua, packed into a small, humidified room.

Cravaterie Nazionali

Valaorítou 5 ☎210 36 20 996. Small but stylish tie boutique, with a fine collection.

Enny di Monaco

Irodótou 18 ☎210 72 17 215. Occasionally eccentric, avant-garde clothing shop; the high-fashion labels include Cesare Fabbri, Adam Jones, Luella and Diana von Furstenberg.

Fresh Line

Skoufá 10 ☎210 36 44 015. Cosmetics store, selling hand-made soaps made from Greek herbs such as nettle, thyme and saffron.

Galerie Zamboulaki

Háritos 26 ☎210 72 52 488. Old furniture and modern art make this place perfect for browsing; you'll find everything from used monastery tables to embroidery.

Giorgos Eleftheriadis

Pindárou 38 ☎210 36 15 278. A great little boutique from a fine Greek designer. Styles are avant-garde – European in cut but essentially Greek in style.

Gucci

Melathron Centre, Tsakálof 5 ☎210 36 02 280. A Gucci boutique in the heart of Kolonáki, with clothes, bags and accessories.

Kanari 5

Kánari 5 ☎210 33 92 597. A mixed bag here, with clothes, shoes, accessories, cosmetics and CDs sharing the same spacious display area. Very chic and aesthetically progressive, with a hairdressing salon on the second floor.

Oikos

Irodótou 26 ☎210 72 31 350. Interesting gifts or just items to scatter around your lounge, – the large collection of gadgets and *objets* makes for a refreshing change from tourist trinkets.

To Paleopoleion

Irodhótou 18 ☎210 72 43 922. Fine old French and Greek furniture and antiques, including porcelain and perfume bottles.

Petai Petai

Skoufá 30 ☎210 36 24 315. A jewellery store with a large collection garnered from Greek designers, featuring exquisite handcrafted silver, gold and precious stones.

Petridis

Plateía Kolonakíou 7 ☎210 72 38 434. Long-established and producing some of the best Greek-made shoes in the country. In addition you'll find men's and women's ranges from Charles Jourdan, Camper, Parallele and other top-line shoemakers.

This 'n' That

Levéndi 7 ☎210 72 93 790. A touch of the Orient, with ethnic fashions, kaftans, sandals and shawls.

Restaurants

Agrio Rodho

Sarandapíhou 15–17 ☎210 36 36 337. Closed Sun. A good place for a post-Lykavitós theatre meal. Food is homely as opposed to haute cuisine, plus game is also on the menu.

Central

Plateía, Kolonakíou ☎210 72 45 938. This fairly upmarket and fun-oriented lounge-bar-cum-restaurant does a funky twist on modern Greek fare, serving a good selection of salads and decent sushi.

Cilentio

Mantzárou 3 & Sólonos ☎210 36 33 144. Serving modern Mediterranean and Greek fusion dishes, this upmarket and fairly costly eatery in an old restored building combines charm with rusticity. Many of the house ingredients are organic.

Dhimokritos

Dhimokrítou 23 ☎210 36 13 588. Closed Sun. Occasionally snooty – but good-value – restaurant in a beautiful Neoclassical building with high ceilings and classy interior decor. The vast menu includes well-prepared dishes such as rabbit in lemon sauce, fish soup, and cabbage *dolmádhes* with lamb.

Filippou

Xenokrátous 19 ☎210 72 16 390. Closed Sat eve & Sun. This conservative

▲ PLATÍA KOLONAKÍOU

taverna, favourite of office workers and residents, is liveliest at lunch. The food is fresh and moderately priced, and includes good grills, stews and casseroles.

47 Maritsa's

Voukourestíou 47 ☎210 36 30 132. Fairly expensive restaurant with a posh interior and pavement seating. Specializes in seafood like monkfish, crayfish fritters, lobster spaghetti and grilled mussels.

Fourtouna

An. Polémou 22 ☎210 72 21 282. The best place for quality seafood in Kolonáki, serving moderately expensive, well-prepared fish. The grilled or steamed crayfish is a speciality; dishes are displayed in a wooden boat in the front area. There's also a buffet range, and a decent wine list which includes lesser-known vintages from Macedonia and the islands.

Ikio

Ploútarhou 15 ☎210 72 59 216. As the restaurant name (meaning "homely") suggests, Ikio is an unfussy taverna with a wide range of oven-baked dishes and salads that don't dent a huge hole in your wallet.

To Kioupi

Platía Kolonakíou 4 ☎210 36 14 033. Closed Sun. A budget subterranean taverna with good, standard Greek fare such as *moussakás* and *dolmádhes*.

Rodhia

Aristíppou 44 ☎210 72 29 883. Closed Sun. Popular taverna set in a cosy old house – the menu hasn't changed in twenty years, but that doesn't bother its many loyal regulars. Favourites include beef in lemon sauce, lamb fricassee and octopus in mustard sauce, while the prices go fairly easy on your pocket.

Rooms

Kriezótou 11 ☎210 36 15 628. A mid-priced newcomer to the Kolonáki culinary scene, *Rooms* is a bit of everything: delicatessen, sushi bar, café and even cigar bar. Very popular with the local trendies.

Sale & Pepe

Aristíppou 34 ☎210 72 34 102. Closed Sun. Good-quality but fairly pricey Italian fare come to town in the form of *Sale & Pepe*, high up on the flanks of Lykavitós Hill. The menu is simple yet hearty and the wine list is most impressive.

Ta Skalakia

Eyinítou 32, Ilísia, off some stairs behind the Holiday Inn ☎210 72 29 290. *Ta Skalakia* is not as cheap or unpretentious as it once was, but still has many classic taverna dishes and attracts a lively crowd.

Bars

Alekos Island

Tsakálof 42. Daily 11pm–3am. Long-established, easy-going basement gay bar playing rock and pop music; Alekos is one of Athens' more colourful bartenders.

Baila

Háritos 43 ☎210 72 33 019. Opens 12.30am. More of a socializing hangout than a full-on bar, with drinks and coffees; the music is low-key, and patrons often gather on the pavement.

City

Háritos 43 ☎210 72 28 910. Opens 9pm. Artists and wannabes hang out here, where sipping drinks takes precedence over the light, discreet music.

Clubs

Café Alu

Skoufá & Omírou 58 ⓣ210 36 11 116. Opens 10pm. Upbeat venue, hosting guest DJs playing mainly modern music.

Memphis

Vendíri 5, Ilísia, behind Hilton Hotel. Roomy, comfy club/bar with a garden and a good sound system pumping out rock and dance.

Mommy

Delfón 4 ⓣ210 36 19 682. Opens 10pm. One of Kolonáki's better meeting places, this is a trendy watering hole for thirty-somethings where soulful house is pumped out by resident DJs.

Live music

Hi-Hat Café

Dhragoúmi 28 and Krousóvou 1, Ilísia nr Hilton Hotel ⓣ210 72 18 171. Crowded, energetic bar that plays mainly blues music, but also features Latin and jazz.

Kriti

Ayíou Thomá 8, Ambelókipi ⓣ210 77 58 258. Closed Mon. Live music venue specializing in Cretan music.

La Joya

Tsóha 43, Ambelókipi ⓣ210 64 40 030. Open until 2.30am. Successful venue with a great atmosphere, beautiful decor and adventurous food; it's popular with celebrity parties. The music is rock, jazz and Latin.

Lykavitós Theatre

Lykavitós Hill. Spectacular outdoor venue used mainly for music concerts from May to October.

Palenque

Farandáton 41, Platía Ay. Thomá, Ambelókipi ⓣ210 64 87 748. Live Latin music by South American groups, as well as salsa parties, flamenco music and dance lessons.

Tsai stin Sahara

Laodhikías 18, Ilísia. Admission and first drink €12. Local venue that often hosts enjoyable Greek folk nights.

Sýndagma and around

All roads lead to Sýndagma – you'll almost inevitably find yourself here sooner or later for the metro and bus connections. Platía Syndágmatos (Constitution Square), to give it its full name, lies roughly midway between the Acropolis and Lykavitós Hill. With the Greek Parliament building (the Voulí) on its uphill side, and banks, offices and embassies clustered around, it's the heart of Athens politically as well as geographically. The square's name derives from the fact that Greece's first constitution was proclaimed (reluctantly under popular pressure) by King Otho from the palace balcony in 1843. It's still the principal venue for mass demonstrations, and in the run-up to elections the major political parties stage their final campaign rallies here. Vital hub as it is, however, the traffic and the crush mean it's not an attractive place to hang around. Escape comes in the form of the National Gardens, a welcome area of greenery stretching out south from the parliament building and offering a traffic-free route down past the Záppio to Hadrian's Arch and the Temple of Olympian Zeus. In other directions the prime shopping territory of Odhós Ermoú heads west towards Monastiráki, with Pláka and the Acropolis to the southwest; Stadhíou and Panepistimíou head northwest towards Omónia; while to the north and east lies Kolonáki and the embassy quarter.

Hotel Grande Bretagne

Vasiléos Yeoryíou 1 ⓣ210 33 30 000, ⓦgrandebretagne.gr. With the exception of the Voulí, the vast Hotel Grande Bretagne – Athens' grandest – is just about

▼ PARLIAMENT BUILDING

the only building on Sýndagma to have survived postwar development. Past the impressive facade and uniformed doormen, the interior is magnificently opulent, as befits a grand hotel established in the late nineteenth century – it's worth taking a look inside, or having a drink at one of the bars. There's a rooftop pool, bar and restaurant, all with great views across the city.

The hotel has long been at the centre of Greek political intrigue: in one notorious episode, Winston Churchill narrowly avoided being blown up here on Christmas Day 1944, when saboteurs from the Communist-led ELAS resistance movement placed a huge explosive charge in the drains. According to whom you believe, the bomb was either discovered in time by a kitchen employee, or removed by ELAS themselves when they realized

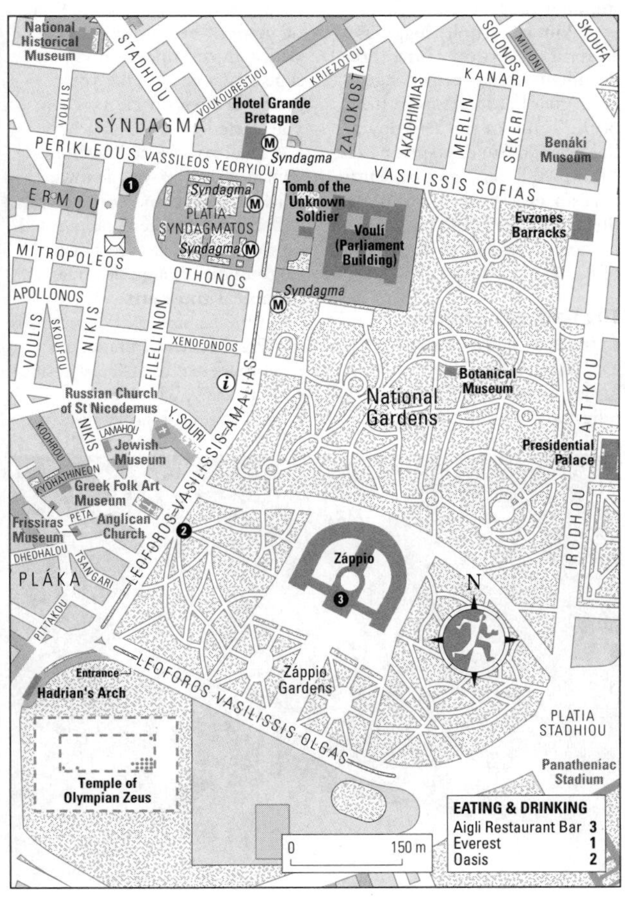

that Churchill was one of their potential victims.

The Voulí

Platía Syndágmatos. Not open to the public. The Greek National Parliament, the Voulí, presides over Platía Syndágmatos from its uphill (east) side. A vast, ochre-and-white Neoclassical structure, it was built as the royal palace for Greece's first monarch, the Bavarian King Otho, who established his capital in Athens and moved in in 1842. In front of it, goose-stepping *evzónes* in tasselled caps, kilt and woolly leggings – a prettified version of traditional mountain costume – change their guard at intervals in front of the Tomb of the Unknown Soldier. On Sundays, just before 11am, a full band and the entire corps parade from the tomb to their barracks at the back of the National Gardens to the rhythm of camera shutters.

The National Gardens

Entrances on Amalías, Vasilíssis Sofías, and Iródhou Attikoú. Daily sunrise–sunset. Free. The most refreshing acres in the city are the National Gardens – not so much a flower garden as a luxuriant tangle of trees, whose shade, benches and duck ponds provide palpable relief from the heat in summer. It's a great spot for a picnic. The gardens were originally the private palace gardens, a pet project of Queen Amalia in the 1840s; supposedly the main duty of the tiny Greek navy in its early days was fetching rare plants, often the gifts of other royal houses, from remote corners of the globe. Despite a major pre-Olympics clear-out, there's still something of an air of benign neglect here, with rampant undergrowth and signs that seem to take you round in circles back to where you started.

A small **zoo** (signed *Irattikou*) contains ostriches, exotic fowl, chickens, rabbits and domestic cats, and there's a children's playground on the Záppio side. Occupying an elegant little pavilion nearby is a **botanical museum**.

On the far side of the gardens is the **Presidential Palace**, the royal residence until Constantine's exile in 1967, where more *evzónes* stand on sentry duty.

▲ THE NATIONAL GARDENS

▲ THE ZÁPPIO

The Záppio

Open 24hr. On the southern side of the National Gardens are the graceful, crescent-shaped grounds of the Záppio. Popular with evening and weekend strollers, they're more open, and more formally laid out. The Záppio itself, an imposing Neoclassical edifice originally built as an exhibition hall, is not open to the public. Although it has no permanent function, the building has taken on prestigious roles such as the headquarters for both the Greek presidency of the European Union and for the people who ran the 2004 Olympic bid.

Hadrian's Arch

Hadrian's Arch stands in splendid isolation on what feels like one of the busiest corners in Athens, where Odhós Syngroú arrives in the centre of town. With the traffic roaring by, this is not somewhere you are tempted to linger – but it's definitely worth a look on your way to the Temple of Olympian Zeus.

The arch, eighteen metres tall, was erected by the emperor to mark the edge of the Classical city and the beginning of his own. On the west side its frieze is inscribed "This is Athens, the ancient city of Theseus", and on the other "This is the City of Hadrian and not of Theseus". With so little that's ancient remaining around it, this doesn't make immediate sense, but you can look up, westwards, to the Acropolis and in the other direction see the columns of the great temple completed by Hadrian. Many more Roman remains are thought to lie under the Záppio area, and over towards the old Olympic Stadium.

▼ HADRIAN'S ARCH

The Temple of Olympian Zeus

Entrance on Vasilíssis Ólgas. Daily: April–Sept 8am–7pm; Oct–March 8.30am–3pm. €2, or joint Acropolis ticket. The colossal pillars of the Temple of Olympian Zeus – also known as the Olympieion – stand in the middle of a huge, dusty clearing with excellent views of the Acropolis. One of the largest temples in the ancient world – according to Livy "the only temple on earth to do justice to the god" – its construction was begun by the tyrant Peisistratos as early as the sixth century BC, but only completed almost seven hundred years later under Hadrian. It was finally dedicated in 131 AD, an occasion that Hadrian marked by contributing an enormous statue of Zeus and an equally monumental one of himself, although both have since been lost. Just fifteen of the temple's original 104 marble pillars remain erect, though the massive column drums of another, which fell in 1852, litter the ground. To the north of the temple enclosure, by the site entrance, are various excavated remains including an impressive Roman bath complex and a gateway from the wall of the Classical city. The south side of the enclosure overlooks a futher area of excavation (not open to the public) where both Roman and much earlier buildings have been revealed.

Cafés

Everest

Ermoú 2, Platía Sindágmatos. Daily 24 hr. With an Easy Internet Café upstairs, this branch of the sandwich chain is always busy. While you can eat in, you may prefer to collect a picnic to take to the National Gardens.

Oasis

West side of National Gardens, opposite cnr of Amalías and Filellínon. This café just off the main avenue is an unexpected haven, offering ice cream, ouzo and *mezédhes* in the shade.

Restaurants

Aigli Restaurant Bar

Záppio Gardens ☎210 33 69 363. Pricey, smart restaurant with a fabulous setting, the haunt of politicians and diplomats. The food is "modern Mediterranean", which here means Greek with French and Italian influences.

▼ TEMPLE OF OLYMPIAN ZEUS

Mets, Pangráti and Koukáki

For a taste of old Athens, head along to Mets, a steep hillside area with almost-intact streets of pre-World War II houses. With their tiled roofs, shuttered windows and courtyards with spiral metal staircases and potted plants, they offer an intimate glimpse at the more traditional side of the city, and it's here, around Márkou Mousoúrou and Arhimídhous, that you'll find the city's most authentic tavernas and bars. The residential district of Pangráti, too, has a wealth of small, homely tavernas and *mezhedopoleía*: Platía Plastíra, Platía Varnáva and Platía Pangratíou are the focal points, the first with a large, old-fashioned *kafeníon* where you can sit for hours on a leafy terrace for the price of a coffee. Several other fine tavernas lie tucked away on and around Platía Varnáva and nearby Odhós Arhimídhous: the latter also holds an impressive street market every Friday. More places to eat lie down towards Leofóros Vasiléos Konstandínou; while you're there it's worth taking a look at nearby Odhós Ágras, an attractive stepped street where Nobel-laureate poet George Seferis once lived.

Pangráti is also where you'll find the original Olympic Stadium, which occupies an impressive spot next to Ardhittós Hill, as well as Athens' First Cemetery, where lie the much-visited tombs of many of the country's luminaries.

Koukáki, huddled close around the southern slopes of Filopáppou Hill, is another district that sees few tourists yet lies in close proximity to the slopes of the Acropolis and the theatres of Dionysos and Herodes Atticus. Tranquil and shady, with tree-lined streets, it's another place that's great for eating and drinking.

You can reach all three areas on foot from the centre, but if you don't fancy the stroll you can hop on to a #2, #4 or #12 trolley to Platía Plastíra, or use the very handy Akrópoli or Syngroú-Fix metro stations.

▲ PANGRÁTI

▲ THE OLD OLYMPIC STADIUM

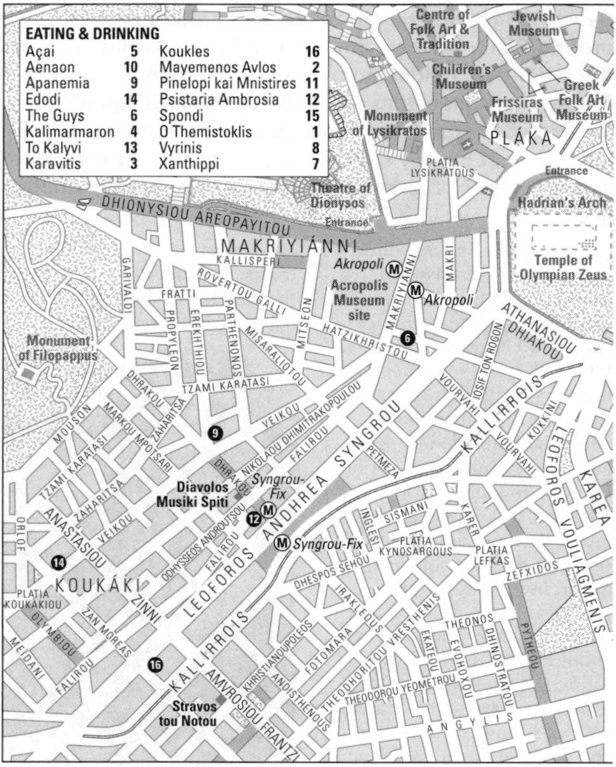

EATING & DRINKING

Açai	5	Koukles	16
Aenaon	10	Mayemenos Avlos	2
Apanemia	9	Pinelopi kai Mnistires	11
Edodi	14	Psistaria Ambrosia	12
The Guys	6	Spondi	15
Kalimarmaron	4	O Themistoklis	1
To Kalyvi	13	Vyrinis	8
Karavitis	3	Xanthippi	7

The Panathenaic Stadium

The old Olympic Stadium (aka the Panathenaic Stadium or the Kalimármaro) is a nineteenth-century reconstruction on Roman foundations, slotted tightly in between the pine-covered spurs of Ardhittós Hill.

This site was originally marked out in the fourth century BC for the Panathenaic athletic contests, but in Roman times, as a grand gesture to mark the reign of the emperor Hadrian, it was adapted for an orgy of blood sports, with thousands of wild beasts baited and slaughtered in the arena. The Roman senator Herodes Atticus later undertook to refurbish the 60,000 seats of the entire stadium; the white marble from these was to provide the city with a convenient quarry through the ensuing seventeen centuries.

The stadium's reconstruction dates from the modern revival of the Olympic Games in 1896 and bears witness to the efforts of another wealthy benefactor, the Alexandrian Greek Yiorgos Averoff. Its appearance – pristine whiteness and meticulous symmetry – must be very much as it was when first restored and reopened under Herodes

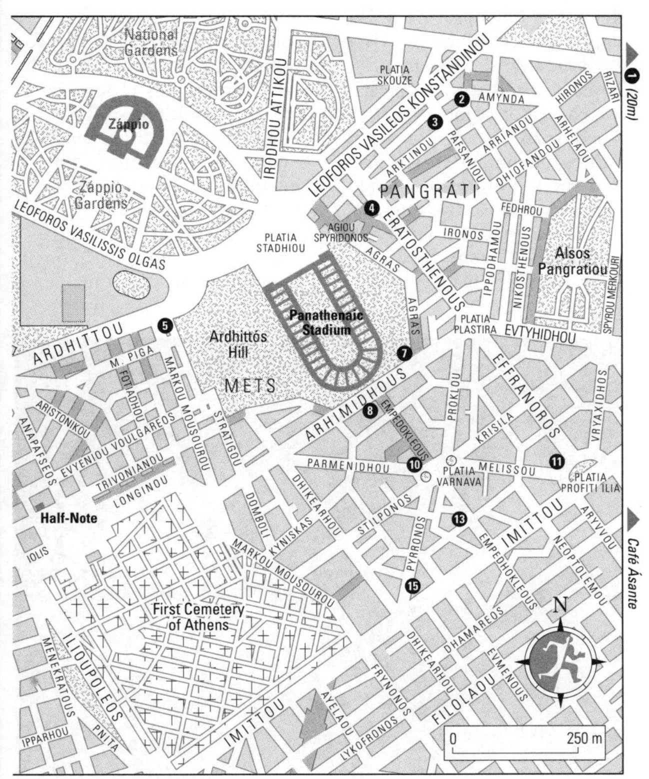

Atticus. It's still used by local athletes and as the finishing point for the Athens Marathon – and indeed for the 2004 Olympic Games marathon.

The River Ilisós and Ardhittós Hill

Few visitors to Athens would be aware of it, but the area bounded by the suburbs of Koukáki, Pangráti and Mets is in fact a river valley through which the River Ilisós once flowed openly. In ancient times the river flowed outside the protective walls of Athens, but nowadays it runs mostly underground. The only section visible to visitors is a small area at the south side of the supporting walls of the Temple of Olympian Zeus. The double sources of this lost river Ilisós are near the Kessarianí monastery and at Karéas near the church of St John the Theologian.

Ilisós, in antiquity, was a demi-god, the son of Poseidon and Demeter, and was worshipped in a sanctuary on Ardhittós Hill next to the Olympic Stadium; several temples, bridges and sanctuaries existed along what was once a bucolic location. Ardhittós Hill is still widely held to be haunted by ancient spirits.

The First Cemetery

The First Cemetery (Próto Nekrotafío) shelters the tombs of just about everybody who was anybody in nineteenth- and twentieth-century Greece, from Heinrich Schliemann to former prime minister Andreas Papandreou. The humbler tombs of musicians, artists and writers are interspersed with ornate mausoleums of soldiers, statesmen and wealthy families, whose descendants come to picnic, stroll and tend the graves. The graveside statuary occasionally attains the status of high art, most notably in the works of Ianoulis Halepas, a *belle époque* sculptor from Tínos. Halepas battled with mental illness for most of his life and died in extreme poverty in 1943; his masterpiece is the idealized *Kimiméni* (Sleeping Girl), on the right about 300m in.

▼ THE FIRST CEMETERY

▲ THE APANEMIA

Restaurants

Aenaon

Plateía Varnáva 9, Pangráti ☎210 70 15 169. Closed Sun. Mid-range place popular for its wine-*mezédhes*, especially the spicy "fire and lava" version. Good draught wine is served, and rebétika sessions take place on Friday and Saturday evenings.

Apanemia

Erekthíou 2 & Veïkou, Koukáki ☎210 92 28 766. Closed Sun. A smart *ouzerí* with a particularly large selection of decently priced *mezédhes*, seafood and fine meat dishes such as pot-roast goat.

Edodi

Veïkou 80, Koukáki ☎210 92 13 013. Eves only, closed Sun. One of Athens' finest restaurants, *Edodi* is a great place for a splurge. The imaginative dishes can be almost dazzling – with prices to match – and include swordfish in a crust of potatoes with mustard sauce, and tart with feta, tomato, aubergine and prosciutto. Waiters will show you all of the various creations before you make a choice.

Karavitis

Pafsaníou 4, Pangráti ☎210 72 15 155. Eves only. A traditional, good-value taverna with draught wine, *mezédhes* and oven-baked main courses. In summer there's outdoor seating in an enclosed garden.

Kalimarmaron

Evforíonos 13 & Eratosthénous, Pangráti ☎210 70 19 727. Closed Mon & Sun. A neat little taverna with a constantly changing menu of carefully prepared and original dishes.

To Kalyvi

Empedhokléous 26, Pangráti ☎210 75 20 641. Eves only, closed June–Sept. A good budget choice, serving excellent, traditional *mezédhes*-type fare. The decor's rustic and they sometimes have live music.

Mayemenos Avlos

Amýnda 4, Pangráti ☎210 72 23 195. The long-established Mayemenos Avlos is one of a trio of small tavernas on this diminutive square. The setting is intimate and the patronage mainly Greek. Serves the usual grills and *mezédhes* at prices that don't hit too hard, and there's occasional live music.

Pinelopi kai Mnistires

Imittoú 130, Pangráti ☎210 75 68 555. Close to Plateía Profiti Ilía, Pinelopi kai Mnistires (Penelope and her Suitors) is a bustling restaurant favoured by Greeks in search of fun and no-nonsense food such as the mid-priced *mousakás* and *souvláki*. There's live music most evenings.

Psistaria Ambrosia

Dhrákou 3–5, Koukáki ☎210 92 20 281. Just up from Syngrou-Fix metro, this popular grill place offers great value on a pedestrian street full of fast-food outlets and small restaurants.

Spondi

Pýrronos 5, Pangráti ☎210 75 20 658. Eves only. A contender for Athens' best restaurant, the swish menu here is French-influenced and is characterized by its combination of simplicity and originality. The dishes include cream of mushrooms with foie gras and truffle, and fillet of sea bass in a fennel, olive-oil and vanilla sauce.

O Themistoklis

Vasiléos Georgíou 31 & Spýrou Merkoúri, Pangráti ☎210 72 19 553. An inexpensive little hole-in-the-wall kind of eatery – known as *koutoúki* in Greek – where the speciality is *bekrí mezés* (meat cubes in a spicy sauce).

Vyrinis

Arhimídhous 11, Pangráti ☎210 70 12 153. Closed Sun. A good, low-key and good-value taverna, with its own house wine and a wide variety of *mezédhes*. There's garden seating in summer.

Xanthippi

Arhimídhous 14 & Ágras, Pangráti ☎210 75 60 514. Just behind the Olympic Stadium and set in a converted old house, *Xanthippi* serves appetizing *mezédhes*, crêpes and meat dishes.

Bars

Açai

Márkou Mousoúrou 1, Mets ☎210 92 37 109. Opens 9pm. €12 entrance on Fri & Sat. A popular venue with the over-thirties, the balcony here has some of the best views of Athens and Lykavittos by night. The music varies from dance to mainstream.

The Guys

Lembési 8, Makriyánni ☎210 92 14 244. Wed–Mon 10pm–3am. A cool, gay lounge-bar where the Greek and international music draws in a mature crowd.

Koukles

Zan Moreás 3, cnr Syngroú, Koukáki ☎210 92 48 989. Wed–Sun only. This gay establishment has the best drag acts in Athens (*Koukles* means "dolls").

Live music

Diavolos Musiki Spiti

Dhrákou 9, Koukáki ☎210 92 39 588. Closed Mon, Tues & May–Sept. Owned by the popular singer Yiannis Glezos, who sometimes puts in an appearance himself, the music here ranges from rebétika to popular in style. The cover charge includes a drink, and on Thursday nights there are tango lessons followed by open dancing.

Café Asante

Damáreos 78, Pangráti ☎210 75 60 102. €6. Expect to see anything from mainstream bands to Afro-Cuban, Indian, Armenian or African outfits, in this excellent, atmospheric venue.

Half-Note

Trivonianoú 17, Mets ☎210 92 13 310. Closed Tues and much of the summer. Good live jazz most nights, often featuring acts from abroad.

Stravos tou Notou

Tharípou 37, Neos Kosmos. One of the liveliest rock clubs in town, featuring mostly Greek acts but with the occasional foreign artist.

Suburban Athens

Athens pushes its suburbs higher and wider each year and all the places covered in this chapter, originally well outside the city, are now approached through a more or less continuous urban landscape. Nonetheless, they variously offer fresh air, seaside settings, and a change of pace from downtown Athens.

The **monasteries of Dhafní** and **Kessarianí**, for example, just half an hour or so from the centre, each retain a definite countryside setting and make for an enjoyable break from the central bustle. Dhafní has world-famous mosaics; while Kessarianí offers exceptional peace and fine walking.

The northern suburb of **Kifissiá**, with its expensive villas, provides an insight into wealthy Athenian life. Its relaxed combination of upmarket shopping and café society, especially busy on Saturdays, can be combined with a visit to the Goulandhrís Natural History Museum and Gaia Centre.

On the coast, **Pireás** and the resort of **Glyfádha** are technically not part of Athens (indeed, Pireás is a proud municipality in its own right). Nevertheless, they too are connected by excellent public transport and by an unbroken ribbon of development. Pireás has ferries to the islands, a couple of good museums and some fine waterfront dining. Glyfádha and the beach suburbs surrounding it are the chief summertime escape for overheating Athenians: not just beaches, but cafés, restaurants, clubs and more shops.

Dhafní

Ierá Odhós, Haïdhari ☎210 58 11 558. Check latest opening details with the tourist office. As well as being a fabulous example of Byzantine architecture at its best, Dhafní Monastery is decorated with mosaics that are considered among the artistic masterpieces of the Middle Ages. The eleventh-century church you see today replaced a fortified fifth-century basilica, which in turn had been adapted from the ruins of a sanctuary of Apollo – the name is derived from the *daphnai* (laurels) sacred to the god. Both the church and the fortifications which enclose it incorporate blocks from the ancient sanctuary; however, the complex has been rebuilt and restored so many times over the years that it's hard to tell what is original.

Dhafní transport

Take bus #A16 or #B16 from Platía Eleftherías, 300m down Pireós from Omónia (Platía Eleftherías is popularly known as Platía Koumoundoúrou and the return buses are so marked); the monastery is to the left of the road, about twenty minutes' ride. Note that the Dhafní metro station is actually in the suburb of Dhafní, on the other side of the city.

Dhafní is easily combined with a visit to Eleusis (see p.137), a further twenty-minute ride on the #A16 bus route.

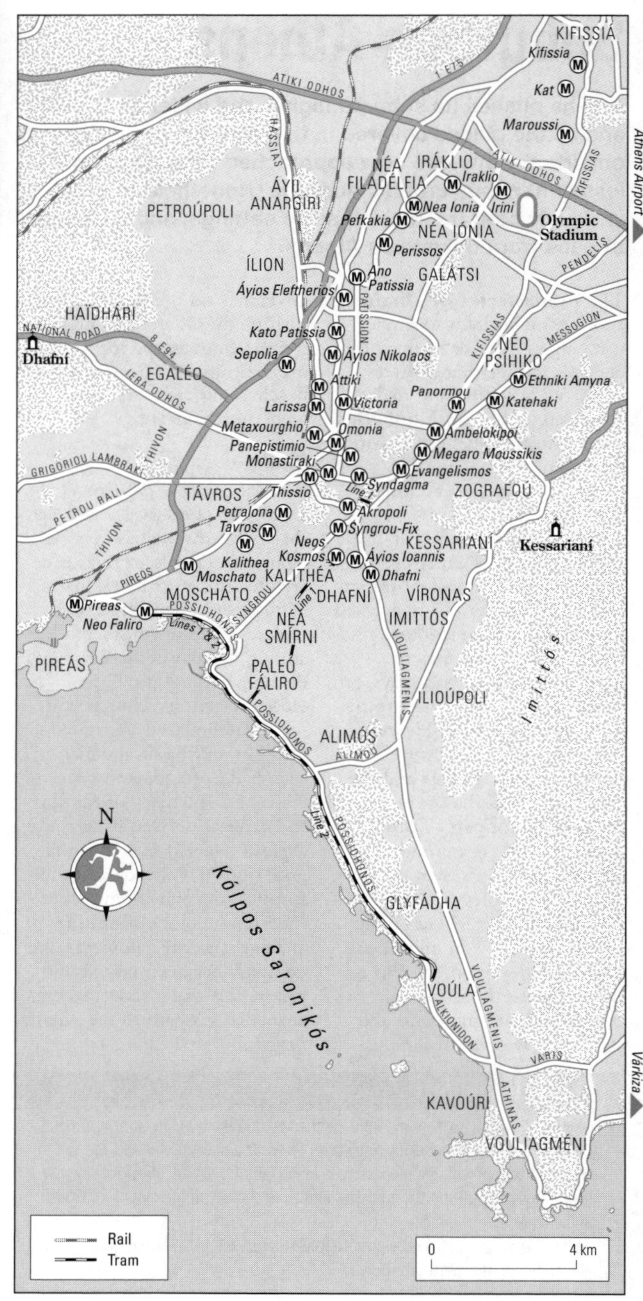
KIFISSIÁ
Kifissia
Kat
Maroussi
Athens Airport
ATIKI ODHOS
E75
NÉA FILADÉLFIA
IRÁKLIO
Iraklio
Irini
Nea Ionia
Olympic Stadium
PETROÚPOLI
ÁYII ANARGÍRI
HASSIAS
Pefkakia
NÉA IÓNIA
Perissos
ÍLION
Ano Patissia
GALÁTSI
PENDELIS
Áyios Eleftherios
PATISSION
HAÏDHÁRI
NATIONAL ROAD
8 E94
Dhafní
Kato Patissia
KIFISSIAS
MESSOGION
NÉO PSÍHIKO
Sepolia
Áyios Nikolaos
Ethniki Amyna
EGALÉO
IERA ODHOS
Attiki
Panormou
Katehaki
Larissa
Victoria
Metaxourghio
Omonia
Ambelokipoi
THIVON
Panepistimio
Megaro Moussikis
Monastiraki
GRIGORIOU LAMBRAKI
Evangelismos
Syndagma
ZOGRAFOÚ
TÁVROS
Thissio
Line 1
PETROU RALI
Petralona
Akropoli
Tavros
Syngrou-Fix
KESSARIANÍ
Kessarianí
Neos Kosmos
Kalithea
Áyios Ioannis
Moschato
KALITHÉA
Dhafni
PIREOS
MOSCHÁTO
SYNGROU
DHAFNÍ
VÍRONAS
Pireas
Neo Faliro
POSSIDHONOS
Line 1
NÉA SMÍRNI
IMITTÓS
Lines 1 & 2
PIREÁS
PALEÓ FÁLIRO
VOULIAGMENIS
ILIOÚPOLI
Imittós
POSSIDHONOS
ALIMÓS
ALIMOU
N
Line 2
Kólpos Saronikós
GLYFÁDHA
VOÚLA
ALKIONIDON
VOULIAGMENIS
VARIS
Várkiza
ATHINAS
KAVOÚRI
VOULIAGMÉNI
Rail
Tram
0
4 km

▼ PANDOKRÁTOR, DHAFNÍ

Inside the church, the celebrated **mosaic cycle** is remarkable for its completeness: there are scenes from the life of Christ and the Virgin, saints, archangels and prophets. The most magnificent is the *Pandokrátor* (Christ in Majesty) on the dome: lit by the sixteen windows of the drum, and set against a background of gold, this stern image directs a tremendous and piercing gaze, his finger poised on the Book of Judgement.

Kessarianí

☎210 72 36 619. Tues–Sun 8am–2.30pm; €2.50. The monastery of Kessarianí is a beautiful and wonderfully peaceful place, just 5km from the centre of the city and yet high enough up the slopes of Mount Imittós to escape the hubbub.

The sources of the River Ilissos provide for extensive **gardens** hereabouts, as they have done since ancient times. Athenians still come to collect water from the local fountains, though these days you're strongly advised not to drink it. The **monastery buildings** date from the eleventh century, though the frescoes in the chapel (a classic cross-in-square design) are much later – executed during the sixteenth and seventeenth centuries. It's a small place, and doesn't take long to see – don't miss the ram's head spouting spring water round the back of the church.

The monastery gardens and the pine-forested slopes around are popular picnic and hiking spots for Athenians. Follow the paths above the monastery, and you'll find a number of chapels and ruined buildings, many of them signposted. From the top – follow signs to Lófos

▼ KESSARIANÍ

Kessarianí transport

Take blue bus #223 or #224 from Akadhimías to the terminus by Kessarianí municipal stadium. From here the monastery is a thirty- to forty-minute climb straight ahead, on a path beside the road up the lower slopes of Mount Imittós.

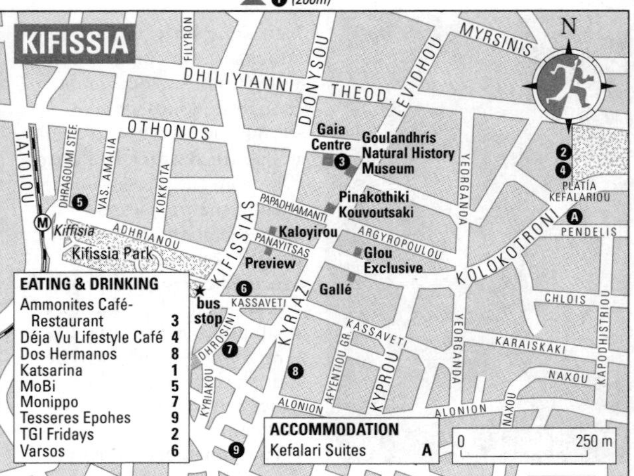

Taxiarchoú – there are wonderful views across Athens to Pireás and the sea beyond, with the Acropolis rising in the foreground.

On the way down you can explore Kessarianí district. Its attractively ramshackle streets don't have anything specifically to seek out, but there are plenty of places to grab a bite or a drink.

Kifissiá

Set on the leafy lower slopes of Mount Pendéli, Kifissiá is one of Athens' swishest suburbs, offering some great designer shopping and a good selection of upmarket eating and drinking options. Its lovely nineteenth-century summer villas and – thanks to the location – the peaceful, cool atmosphere, mean that it comes as a marked change of pace to the vibrancy of the city centre.

Shopping and dining aside, the **Goulandhrís Natural History Museum** (daily except Fri 9am–2.30pm; €3) offers a more cultural excuse to visit. Set in a fine old mansion, the collection has especially good coverage of Greek birds, butterflies and endangered species such as the monk seal and loggerhead sea turtle, plus a 250,000-specimen herbarium. Perhaps more interesting, especially for kids, the adjacent **Gaia Centre** (same hours; €4.50) offers a mildly interactive trip through the natural cycle of the earth and ecological issues (note that labelling is in Greek, so be sure

Kifissiá transport

Kifissiá is the northernmost stop on the metro, 35 minutes or so from Omónia, passing the Olympic site at Iríni along the way. There are also numerous buses, including the #550, which heads through the centre via Syngroú and Vassilísis Sofías, and the #E7, #A7 and #B7, all of which start from Platía Káningos near Omónia.

to get an audio guide). Lastly, the **Pinakothiki Kouvoutsaki** (Tues–Fri 9am–2pm & 6–9pm; Sat & Sun 10am–3pm; free) is a private collection of modern Greek figurative art that's worth a quick look.

Pireás

Pireás has been the port of Athens since Classical times, when the so-called Long Walls, scattered remnants of which can still be seen, were built to connect it to the city. Today it is

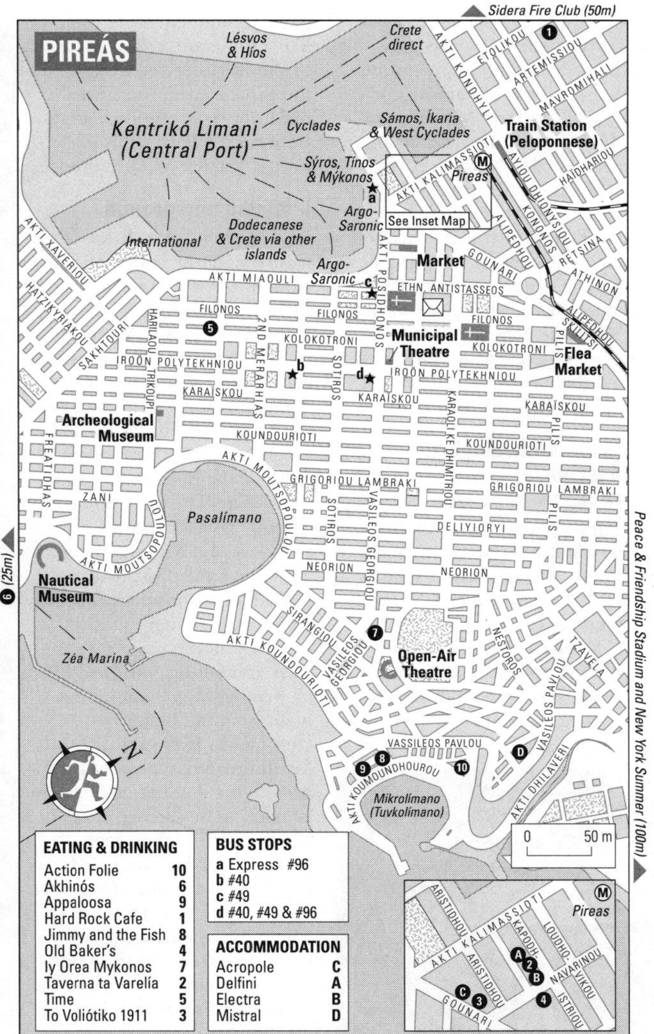

Pireás transport

The metro takes about twenty minutes from Omónia to Pireás. Bus #40 (every 10min 5am–midnight, hourly 1–5am) runs to and from Sýndagma; #49 from Omónia (every 15min 5am–midnight, hourly 1–5am). Bus #904 runs from near the metro to Zéa Marina, trolley-bus #20 to Mikrolímano. Taxis cost €6–7 at day-tariff from the centre of Athens – worth considering, especially if you're heading for Zéa Marina or Mikrolímano, which are a long walk from the metro.

a substantial metropolis in its own right and the port has a gritty fascination of its own, but the real attractions are around the smaller-boat harbours of Zéa Marina and Mikrolímano. Here, the upscale residential areas are alive with attractive waterfront cafés, bars and restaurants. There's also an excellent Archeological Museum and a big Sunday-morning flea market – more an event to experience than a place to shop. Above all, Athenians come to Pireás to eat on the waterfront, and the excellent fish tavernas are packed at weekends.

Pireás Archeological Museum

Hariláou Trikoúpi 31 ☎210 45 21 598. Tues–Sun 8.30am–3pm; €3. An excellent little museum, many of whose displays were dragged from the harbour bed. Specially good are the second-century-AD stone reliefs of battles between Greeks and Amazons, apparently mass-produced for export to Rome; and a huge grave monument that's more like a miniature temple. The star of the show, however, must be the bronze *kouros* (idealized male statue) of Apollo; dating from 530–520 BC, this is the earliest known life-size bronze.

▼ FERRY, PIREÁS

Glyfádha and around

The southern suburbs of Athens form an almost unbroken line along the coast all the way from Pireás to Vouliagméni, some 20km away. This is Athens' summer playground, and the centre of it - for shopping, clubbing, dining or posing on the beach – is **Glyfádha** and its neighbour Voúla. At weekends half of Athens seems to head down here. The epicentre is around the crescent of Leofóros Angélou Metáxa, which curves away from the coast road by Glyfádha's main square. Virtually all the beaches here, and certainly all the more pleasant ones, charge for entry and offer all manner of activities: for a quiet swim it's better to continue to **Kavoúri** or **Vouliagméni**, where you still have to pay but the atmosphere is much more serene. Vouliagméni itself is very upmarket, its beautiful cove beaches a traditional hang-out of Athens' rich and famous. There is also pleasant (and free) swimming to be enjoyed from the rocks between here and the resort of **Várkiza**, the last stop for the local buses.

Glyfádha transport

From central Athens take bus #A2 (which continues to Voúla), #E2 express, #A3 or #B3: all of them leave from Akadhimías. For other beaches along the coast, transfer onto local services #114 (Glyfádha–Kavoúri–Vouliagméni) or #115/6 (Glyfádha–Vouliagméni–Várkiza). The new coastal tram line should also start running in 2004, from Fáliro to Glyfádha.

▲ VOULIAGMÉNI

Shops

Central Prince Oliver

Angélou Metáxa 23, Glyfádha. Upscale designer gear, predominantly for men.

Ensayar

Angélou Metáxa 22 & 24–26, Glyfádha. Men's and women's fashion in two shops (one apiece) from designer names such as Dolce and Gabanna, and Voyage. This street is lined with similar, if less glitzy, places.

Gallé

Kolokotróni 10, Kifissiá. Fashion store with clothing, accessories and shoes from the likes of Paul Smith and Givenchy as well as local designers. Marginally easier on the wallet than neighbours like Gucci and Kenzo.

Glou Exclusive

Koloktróni 9, Kifissiá. In the very heart of the Kifissiá shopping area, this Greek men's fashion chain is reasonably priced, though the *Exclusive* bit of the name indicates that it's only the upper end of their range on offer here.

Kaloyirou

Panayítsas 5, Kifissiá; Kýprou 72, Platía Espéridhon, Glyfádha. Long-established designer shoe store (also with branches downtown). Men's and women's ranges, from Prada to Miu Miu, are stocked.

Li-La-Lo

Grigoríou Lambráki 16, cnr Angélou Metáxa, Glyfádha. Big, glitzy jewellery store specializing in silver.

Preview

Panayítsas 6, Kifissiá. Designer footwear – good range of lesser-known brands, though still expensive.

Cafés

Ammonites Café-Restaurant

Othónos 100, in the Gaia Centré Goulandhrís Museum complex, Kifissiá. Relaxed and luxurious, but the

▲ KIFISSÍA

sandwiches and light meals here come with a hefty price tag.

Déja Vu Lifestyle Café

Platía Kefalaríou, Kifissiá. The name says it all – come here to see and be seen while lingering over your *cappuccino freddo* or salad lunch.

MoBi

Adhrianoú cnr Dhragoúmi, Kifissiá. Right opposite the metro station, this is a handy place to stop for a quick coffee and a sandwich.

Varsos

Kassavéti 5, Kifissiá. This old-fashioned patisserie specializing in home-made yogurts, jams and sticky cakes is a Kifissiá landmark, acting as a meeting place for the whole neighbourhood.

Restaurants

Akhinós

Aktí Themistokléous 51, Pireás ⓣ210 45 26 944. Wonderful seafood and traditional Greek specialities served on a covered terrace overlooking a small beach just round the corner from the Naval Museum. Pricey if you go for the fish, but less so than harbourfront alternatives. Book at weekends.

Akti

Possidhónos 6, Vouliagméni ⓣ210 89 60 448. Taverna right by the sea serving simple, fresh seafood. As ever, fish is expensive but then so is Vouliagméni and by those standards, *Akti* is good value. Waterfront tables are in great demand, so booking is essential.

Al Mawal

Marangoú 18, Glyfádha ⓣ210 89 44 227. The best-value Lebanese restaurant in Glyfádha – authentic food and atmosphere, with belly dancers on Saturday nights.

Beer Garden Ritterburg

Ethnikís Andístasis 214, Kessarianí ⓣ210 72 22 235. Closed Sun. Handily situated right at the top of Kessarianí on the main road, this German-themed places serves Schnitzels, sausages and Bavarian specialities, best sampled on a variety plate.

Buffalo Bill

Kýprou 13, Glyfádha ⓣ210 89 43 128. Eves only, plus Sun lunchtime; closed Sun July–Aug. Get into the Glyfádha mood at this lively, mid-priced Tex-Mex joint. As you'd expect, there are steaks and chilli on offer, plus margaritas by the jugful.

Dos Hermanos

Kyriazí 24, Kifissiá ⓣ210 80 17 337. Closed Mon. Good Mexican food and tasty margaritas in a lively, late-opening bar-restaurant, though with expensive Kifissiá prices.

Hard Rock Cafe

Etolikoú 28 cnr Papastrátou, Pireás ⓣ210 41 36 750. Burgers and beers in what seems an unusual location for a branch of the international chain. In fact, this industrial district behind the port is becoming something of a nightlife hot spot, and this is the place to go before moving on to the clubs.

Island

Limanakia Vouliagménis, km27 on Athens-Soúnio road between Vouliagméni and Várkiza ⓣ210 96 53 563. Summer eves only. *The* place to be seen, this bar-restaurant has a magnificent view (if you get a table at the front), simple island decor, and an international menu at international prices. It serves

▲ MIKROLÍMANO, PIREÁS

everything from sushi to steak, plus fine wines, and you'll need to book.

Jimmy and the Fish

Aktí Koumoundhoúrou 46, Mikrolímano, Pireás ☎210 41 24 417. Excellent, glamorous and inevitably expensive fish taverna occupying the prime position among the harbourside places on Mikrolímano. Booking essential at weekends.

Katsarina

Kifissías 311, Kifissiá ☎210 62 54 072. Closed Wed. Excellent at the basics – grilled meat and plain Greek dishes. There's something of a crowd of (mainly Greek) restaurants on this stretch of Leofóros Kifissías, about 700m north of Platía Platánou.

Masa

Ethnikís Andístasis 240, Kessarianí ☎210 72 36 177. Closed Mon. Straightforward, inexpensive Greek taverna with good, simple food and barrel wines.

Monippo

Dhrosíni 12, Kifissiá ☎210 62 31 440. Wide range of *mezédhes* from all over Greece and smart, modern decor make this a typical Kifissiá hangout. It's better value than most, though, and often has music on Friday and Saturday nights.

Iy Orea Mykonos

Kilkís cnr Sfakión, Kastella, Pireás. The hill above Mikrolímano has great views and many restaurants popular with locals. This simple island-style fish taverna, near the open-air theatre, is one of the best, and significantly cheaper than the same fare on the waterfront.

Sotis

Konstantinoupóleos 9, Glyfádha ☎210 89 42 268. Greek taverna standards at reasonable prices in this elegantly decorated place right at the heart of Glyfádha's restaurant strip, just off the main square.

TGI Fridays

Koloktróni 35, Platía Kefalaríou, Kifissiá ☎210 62 33 947. Archetypal Kifissiá: burgers, ribs and mobile phones all round, but considerably classier than the average branch of this chain.

Time

Skouzé 14, Pireás ☎210 42 85 937. The cosmopolitan nature of Pireás is very much in evidence here: this authentic, inexpensive Indo-Pakistani restaurant caters largely to locals, in the midst of a small ethnic and red-light quarter.

Trata

Platía Anayeníseos 7–9, Kessarianí ☎210 72 91 533. Closed Aug. Well-known fish restaurant on a square with several tavernas just off Ethnikís Andístasis. Fish is always pricey in Athens, but this is good value.

Vincenzo

Yiannitsopoúlou 1, Platía Espéridhon, Glyfádha ☎210 89 41 310. Fine, reasonably priced Italian fare, including excellent pizzas from a wood oven.

To Voliótiko 1911

Goúnari 9, Pireás ☎210 42 25 905. Traditional Greek taverna right in the heart of the port area. Gastronomy isn't this area's forte, but this is good value, and a good option if you're waiting for a ferry.

Bars

Action Folie

Aktí Dhilavéri 9–11, Mikrolímano, Pireás ☎210 41 74 325. Café-bar that's open all day and most of the night, every day. The tables outside make a good place to check out all the action of this buzzing nightlife area.

Appaloosa

Aktí Koumoundoúrou 62, Mikrolímano, Pireás ☎210 42 20 138. A pub-bar that's open all day and late into the night. Terrace seating on the waterfront, and a menu as varied as cheese fondue, souvlaki and spaghetti, plus breakfasts and Murphy's stout.

Sofa Café

Possidhónos 32, Glyfádha ☎210 98 16 092. Tranquil café-bar, with ambient music in the evenings, a popular place to chill out among the big clubs along the seafront boulevard.

Sussex Inn

Dhousmáni 8–10, Glyfádha ☎210 89 41 736. An English Pub right in the heart of Glyfádha – with dartboard, rock music, Caffrey's and a quiz night every Thursday.

Tesseres Epohes

Platía Ayíou Dhimítriou 13, Kifissiá ☎210 80 18 233. An unpretentious little bar where you can enjoy drinks, snacks, and excellent, unamplified live Greek music.

Clubs

New York Summer

Ethnárkhou Makaríou 10, Fáliro, near Stádhio Filías & Irínis ☎210 48 34 190. Oriental in decor, the music remains firmly Western, with popular dance sounds as well as Greek hits.

Sidera Fire Club

Egáleo 21 cnr Mesolongíou, Pireás ☎210 46 12 777. Big club with three bars and a mix of music from Greek to modern dance.

Studio 54

Ríbas 1, Várkiza ☎210 96 56 150. Recently reinventing itself into one of the hot spots in this buzzing seaside suburb, *Studio 54* plays standard dance vibes.

Venue

Km 30 on the Athens–Soúnio road, Várkiza ☎210 89 70 333. *Venue*'s lush setting and eclectic selection of dance music – including some Greek – attracts a young crowd.

Attica

Attica (Attikí), the region encompassing the capital, is not much explored by tourists – only the great romantic ruin of the Temple of Poseidon at Cape Soúnio is well-known. Yet a trip out here makes for a pleasant break, with much of Greece in microcosm to be seen within an hour or two of the capital. There's mountainside at Párnitha, rewarding archeological sites in Brauron and Ramnous, and, if the heat is getting to you, plenty of beaches too. Combine a couple of these with a meal at one of the scores of seaside *psarotavernas* (fish restaurants), always packed out on summer weekends, and you've got a more than worthwhile day out.

Cape Soúnio

A dramatic vantage point from which to look out over the Aegean, Cape Soúnio (Akrotíri Souníou) has for centuries been a landmark for boats sailing between Pireás and the islands. On its tip stands the captivating **Temple of Poseidon** (Tues–Sun 10am–sunset; €5), the heart of what was once a major sanctuary to the sea god. Doric in style, it was built in the time of Pericles, probably by the architect of the Hephaisteion in the Athens Agora. It owes much of its fame to Byron, who visited in 1810, carved his name on the nearest pillar (an unfortunate and much-copied precedent) and immortalized the place in verse. The setting is

Attica transport

Soúnio buses depart on the hour and half-hour from the KTEL terminal on Mavrommatéon at the southwest corner of the Pedhíon Áreos Park; there's also a more central (but in summer, very full) stop ten minutes later on Filellínon, south of Sýndagma at the corner of Xenofóndos. There are both coastal (*paraliakó*) and inland (*mesoyiakó*) services, the latter slightly longer and more expensive. The coast route normally takes around two hours; last departures back to Athens are posted at the Soúnio stop.

There are frequent buses to **Rafína** (40min) and several a day to **Marathónas** (many via the beaches at **Skhiniás**), **Loútsa** and **Pórto Ráfti** (Pórto Ráfti buses sometimes give the final destination as Avláki).

For **Vravróna** it's easiest to go to Loútsa, and then transfer to the local bus that plies up and down the coast road: this bus stops right outside the site (look for the *Club Med*, directly opposite) and terminates just beyond. **Ramnous** is not realistically accessible by public transport, though you should get a lift for the final few kilometres if you take a bus to Ayía Marína (several daily) and hitch from the junction.

Buses to **Párnitha** run from Platía Váthis twice daily, at 6.30am (6.40am weekends) and 2.30pm, with extra services on Sunday at 8am and 3.40pm. Buses to Fylí also leave from Platía Váthis.

For **Eleusis** take bus #A16 from Platía Eleftherías, on Pireós. Ask to be dropped at the "Heroön" (Sanctuary), to the left of the main road, a short way into Elefsína. A trip to Eleusis is easily combined with Dhafní (p.123), which you pass on the way.

▲ CAPE SOÚNIO

wonderful – on a clear day the view takes in the islands of Kéa, Kýthnos and Sérifos to the southeast, Égina and the Peloponnese to the west – and the temple's picturesque semi-ruined state makes this as evocative a site as any in Greece. Come early or late, though, if you want to avoid the crowds.

The rest of the site is of more academic interest. There are remains of a fortification wall around the sanctuary; a *propylaion* (entrance hall) and *stoa*; cuttings for two shipsheds; and the foundations of a small Temple of Athena. The port of **Lávrio**, a little further round the coast, has numerous cafés and restaurants, as well as a one-room Archeological Museum (Mon & Wed–Sun 10am–3pm; free) with finds from the site.

The east coast: Rafína to Pórto Ráfti

The east coast is a favourite weekend and holiday escape for

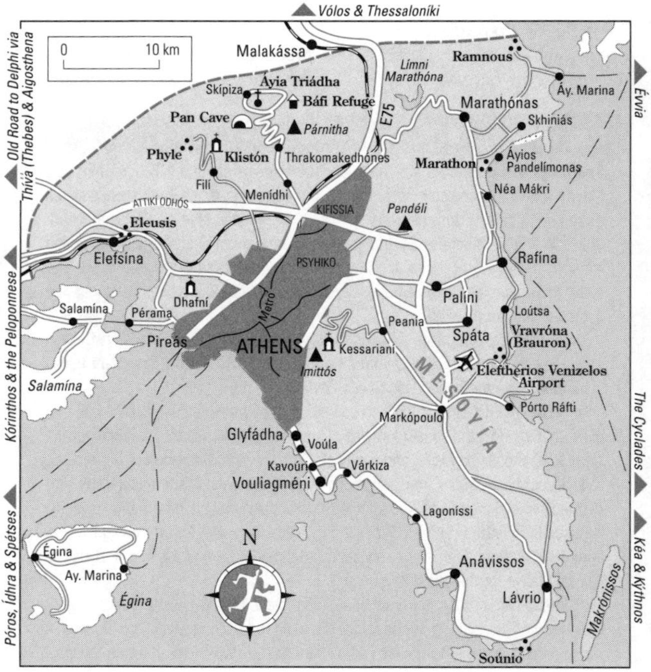

▲ FERRY, RAFÍNA

jaded Athenians. The main route out of the city heads straight for the little port of **Rafína**, from where you can head off to numerous islands, including nearby Évvia. Boats aside, the appeal of the place is mainly gastronomic: the little fishing harbour's line of roof-terrace seafood restaurants is one of the most inviting spots on Attica's coast, with views of the comings and goings of the port a free extra.

There are local beaches in easy walking distance, and others, all with more seafront dining, further away along the coast. To the north, en route to Marathon or Ramnous, **Néa Mákri** lies at the heart of a string of small beach developments. South, there's continual development down through **Loútsa** to Vravróna (p.136). **Pórto Ráfti**, just beyond, is more attractive, with a scattering of popular waterfront restaurants and, in summer, a thriving nightlife scene.

Marathon

The site of the most famous and arguably most important military victory in Athenian history is not far from the village of **Marathónas**, 42km from Athens. Here, in 490 BC, a force of 9000 Athenians and 1000 of their Plataian allies defeated a Persian army 25,000 strong. After the victory a runner was sent to Athens to declare the news: having run the first marathon, he delivered his message and dropped dead. Just 192 Athenians died in the battle (compared to some 6000 Persians), and the burial mound where they were laid, the **Týmvos Marathóna** (Tues–Sun 8.30am–3pm; €3), can still be seen, off the road between Rafína and Marathónas. Consisting only of overgrown earth piled ten metres high, now rather overgrown and neglected, it is a quietly impressive monument. The **Mound of the Plataians**, where the eleven Plataians (including a ten-year-old boy) who died were laid to rest, is about 5km away near the edge of the mountain; there's also an **archeological museum** here (Tues–Sun 8.30am–3pm; €3), with a sparse collection of artefacts, mainly from the local Cave of Pan, a deity felt to have aided the victory.

Marathónas village itself has plenty of places to eat, but there are many more attractive options if you head for the coast.

Skhiniás

Skhiniás, a long, pine-backed strand with shallow water, is one of the best free beaches within easy reach of Athens. Big enough to allow some chance of escaping the crowds, its southern parts are relatively developed, with a number of cordoned-off pay-beach sections and beach clubs offering showers, umbrellas and watersports. Further north there's far less development apart from scattered tavernas on the sand.

Ramnous

Summer Mon 12.30–7pm, Tues–Sun 8am–7pm; winter Tues–Sun 8.30am–3pm. €2. The little-visited ruins of Ramnous (Ramnoúndas) occupy an isolated, atmospheric hillside site with magnificent views steeply down to the sea and across the strait to Évvia. The site was an Athenian lookout point from the earliest times, and remains of walls and fortifications can clearly be seen continuing way below the fenced site, all the way down to the rocky shore.

Within the site, the principal ruin is a Doric **Temple of Nemesis**, goddess of divine retribution. Pausanias records that the Persians incurred her wrath by their presumption in bringing with them to Greece a giant marble block upon which they intended to commemorate their victory. They met their nemesis, however, at the battle of Marathon, and the Athenians used the marble to create a statue instead. There are also the remains of a smaller temple dedicated to Themis, goddess of justice, and a section of ancient road.

Vravróna

Site & museum summer Mon 12.30–7pm, Tues–Sun 8am–7pm; winter Tues–Sun 8.30am–3pm. €3. Ancient Vravróna, also known as Brauron, is one of the most enjoyable minor Greek sites. The remains, centred on a vast *stoa*, are of a Sanctuary of Artemis, goddess of hunting and childbirth, and protector of new-born children. Vravróna was the chief site of the Artemis cult, which staged an important festival every four years. This featured a procession from Athens and other rites, now shrouded in mystery, in which young girls dressed as bears to enact a ritual connected with the goddess and childbirth.

The **Stoa of the Bears**, where these initiates stayed, has been substantially reconstructed, along with a stone bridge; both are fifth century BC. Somewhat scantier are the ruins of the temple itself, whose stepped foundations can be made out; immediately adjacent, the sacred spring still wells up, squirming with tadpoles in spring. Nearby, steps lead up to a chapel which contains some damaged frescoes.

The site – frequently waterlogged – overlooks a marshy bay, which comes alive

▲ RAMNOUS

▲ FORTRESS AT PHYLE

early in the morning and late at night with birdsong and the croaking of frogs. The site **museum** lies down here, a good 2km away by road. Various finds from the sanctuary are displayed, including some marble heads modelled after the little girls, and bear-masks.

Mount Párnitha and Phyle

Scarcely an hour's bus ride from Athens' city centre, Mount Párnitha is an unexpectedly vast and virgin tract of forest, rock and ravine. It will give you a taste of what Greek mountains are all about, including a good selection of mountain flowers. The trip is especially worthwhile in March or April, when snow lies surprisingly late on the north side and, in its wake, carpets of crocus, alpine squills and mountain windflower spring from the mossy ground, while lower down you'll find aubretia, tulips, dwarf iris and a whole range of orchids. Much of the mountain is now a National Park, and there are numerous waymarked paths on the mountain (look for red discs and multicoloured paint splodges on the trees). The principal ones are the approach to the Báfi refuge up the Hoúni ravine, and the walk to the Skípiza spring. Another highly evocative spot for lovers of classical ghosts is the **Cave of Pan**, which Menander used as the setting for one of his plays. The best approach is by track and trail from the chapel of Ayía Triádha, 2.3km west of the top station of the Mount Párnitha télephérique. A topographical map showing local landmarks (labelled in Greek) is posted just behind the church.

The mountain is also home to the ruined but still impressive fourth-century-BC Athenian fort of **Phyle**, about an hour and three-quarters on foot beyond the village of Fylí (known locally as Khasiá) via the restored fourteenth-century **monastery of Klistón**. **Fylí** itself is a popular country culinary outing for Athenians with lots of family-style tavernas and restaurants.

Note that roads on Párnitha are notoriously bereft of signposts – so if you're driving, Road Editions' 1:50,000 *Párnitha* **map** is highly recommended.

Eleusis (Elefsína)

Tues–Sun 8.30am–3pm. €3. The **Sanctuary of Demeter** at Eleusis, on the edge of the modern town of Elefsína, at the beginning of the Sacred Way to Athens, was one of the most important in the ancient Greek world. For two millennia, the ritual ceremonies known as the Mysteries were performed here. The ruins of the sanctuary, however, though extensive, date from several different ages of rebuilding and are largely reduced to foundations. It's hard

The Mysteries of Eleusis

The ancient Mysteries had an effect on their initiates equal to that of any modern cult. According to Pindar, who experienced the rites in Classical times and, like all others, was bound on pain of death not to reveal their content, anyone who has "seen the holy things [at Eleusis] and goes in death beneath the earth is happy, for he knows life's end and he knows the new divine beginning."

Established in Mycenaean times, perhaps as early as 1500 BC, the cult centred around the figure of Demeter, the goddess of corn, and the myth of her daughter Persephone's annual descent into and resurrection from the underworld, which came to symbolize the rebirth of the crops (and the gods responsible for them) and the miracle of fertility.

By the fifth century BC the cult had developed into a sophisticated annual festival, attracting up to 30,000 people from all over the Greek world. Participants gathered in Athens, outside the Propylaia on the Acropolis, and, after various rituals, including mass bathing and purification in the sea at Fáliro, followed the Sacred Way to the sanctuary here at Eleusis. One theory suggests that one of the rituals entailed drinking a potion containing grain-ergot fungus, producing similar effects to those of modern psychedelic drugs. The Mysteries survived well into the Christian era, but eventually fell victim to the new orthodoxy.

to work out what's what, so the best plan is to head for the museum, which features models of the sanctuary at various stages in its history and some excellent finds from the site. This will point you in the direction of the most important of the remains, the **Telesterion**. This windowless Hall of Initiation lay at the heart of the cult: it was here that the priests of Demeter would exhibit the "Holy Things" – presumably sheaves of fungus-infected grain, or vessels containing the magic potion – and speak "the Unutterable Words" whilst under their hallucinogenic influence.

▲ ELEUSIS

Restaurants

Akriogiali

Just before the turn-off for the Aigeo hotel, Soúnio ☎229 20 39 107. Oct–April closed eves. This blue-and-white taverna has both character and history – a number of illustrious Greek guests have dined here. The food, mainly fish, is simple but cooked to perfection.

I Avli tou Antoni

Nikoláou Plastíra 10, Néa Mákri ☎229 40 97 709. Fri–Sun eves only. Excellent home-made *mezédhes* and *mayireftá*, moderately priced.

I Avra

Limáni, Rafína ☎229 40 91 598. Set on the harbour, *I Avra* serves pricey but well-prepared grilled fish and salads that even feature fresh coriander, otherwise a rarity in Greece.

Farangi

Leofóros Fylís, Fylí ☎210 24 11 475. Moderately priced, hearty grills and *mezédhes* are the order of the day here.

Ioakeim

Limáni, Rafína ⓣ229 40 23 421. One of the better harbour tavernas, with prices that reflect this, *Ioakeim* has been around for over fifty years. Fish features in the main, but try the wild leaf salads or seaweed in season; there's also excellent pickled octopus.

Kali Kardia

Just behind the Town Hall, Kostí Palamá 12, Rafína ⓣ229 40 23 856. Mon–Thurs eves only, Fri, Sat & Sun all day. The inexpensive *Kali Kardia* specializes in grills, with excellent beef patties and spare ribs.

Kavouri

Perikléous 24, Paralía Marathóna ⓣ22940 55243. Mainly fish, with a smattering of moderately priced grilled meats and various *mezédhes*.

Psarotaverna Paradhosiako

Paralía, Lávrio ⓣ229 20 60 841. Right on the waterfront, the excellent fish served here comes straight from the boats – though as ever, it's not cheap.

Psaropoula-Bibikos

Leofóros Avlakíou 118, Pórto Ráfti ⓣ229 90 71 292. A good fish taverna, also serving grilled meats and a few *mayireftá* dishes, at prices that won't break the bank.

▼ TAVERNA, LÁVRIO

Rombolo

Leofóros Marathónos, a little way out of Rafína on the way to Marathon ⓣ229 40 32 900. Closed eves & Mon. This mid-range, family-style restaurant has live music on Friday, Saturday and Sunday.

Sta Kala Kathoumena

Vasiléos Georgíou 8, Rafína ⓣ229 40 25 688. The moderately priced dishes show a marked home-cooking bent and include Constantinopolitan dishes such as *gardhoúmbes* (entrail sausages) and *pastourmadhélia* (smoked and spiced meat wedges).

Syrtaki

Soúnio ⓣ229 20 39 125. Close to the ancient site and with a stunning view, this simple taverna serves traditional dishes in which fish features predominantly.

Tria Adhelfia

Paralía Marathóna ⓣ229 40 56 461. A decent waterside taverna on the beach at Marathon, with middling prices.

Vrakha

Leofóros Plákas 99, Lávrio ⓣ229 20 27 745. A good, inexpensive place to sample suckling pig and lamb cooked in vine leaves, or a wide range of *mayireftá*.

Xypolitos

25th Martíou & Georgíou Papadópoulou 1, Loútsa ⓣ229 40 28 342. Mon–Fri eves only, Sat & Sun all day. *Xypolitos* is one of the oldest and best fish tavernas along the coast, although it's a little pricey.

Further afield

With the use of a hire car or by taking one of many tours available out of Athens, you can visit a wealth of sites and attractions, all within a few hours' reach. Highlights include the stunning ruins of Delphi (site of the famous Delphic Oracle in ancient times), mountain hiking on the slopes of Mount Parnassós and the impressive ancient sites of Tiryns and Mycenae. From the port of Pireás, too, you can easily jump on a comfortable ferry or fast hydrofoil and be on a Greek island in the Argo-Saronic gulf within an hour or two, making for some wonderfully varied day-trips – although you may want to enjoy longer outings by taking advantage of the countless places to stay you'll find everywhere you go.

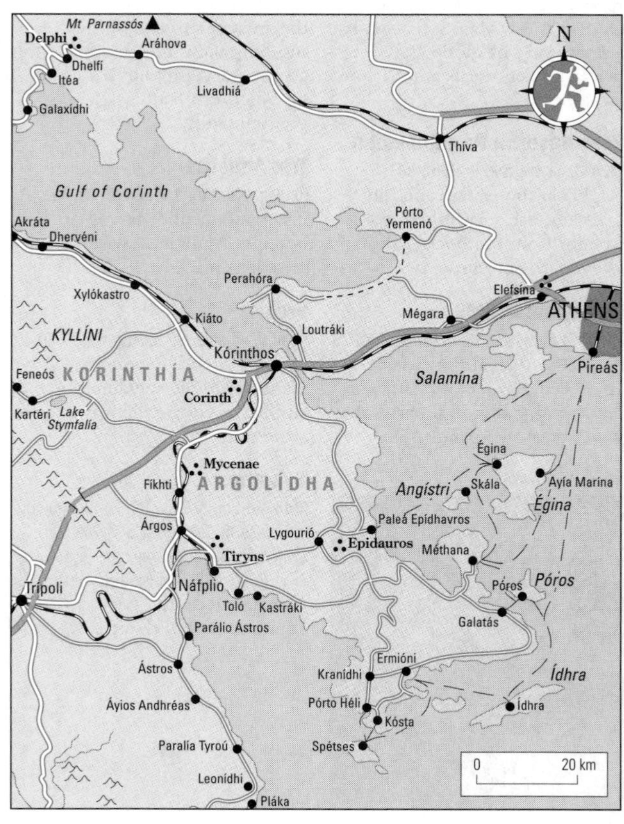

▼ THOLOS, DELPHI

Delphi

Sacred Precinct daily: summer 7.30am–7pm; winter 8am–5pm; €6, or €9 joint ticket with museum. Museum summer: Mon–Fri 7.30am–6.45pm, Sat & Sun 8.30am–2.45pm; winter daily 8.30am–2.45pm. €6, or €9 joint ticket with site. Sanctuary of Athena daily: summer 8am–7pm; winter 8am–5pm; free. With its site raised on the slopes of a high mountain terrace and dwarfed to either side by the massive crags of Mount Parnassós, it's easy to see why the ancients believed Delphi to be the centre of the earth. As if the natural setting and occasional earthquake and avalanche weren't enough to confirm a divine presence, this, according to Plutarch, was where a rock chasm was discovered that exuded strange vapours and reduced people to frenzied, incoherent and prophetic mutterings. Thus was born the famous **Delphic Oracle**, to which kings and simple citizens flocked in an attempt to forsee their future.

Delphi is a large and complex ruin, best taken in two stages, with the sanctuary and precinct ideally at the beginning or end of the day, or (in winter) at lunchtime, to escape the crowds.

The **Sacred Precinct** contains most of the sights – including the Temple of Apollo, the impressive theatre and the stadium. The Marmaria, or **Sanctuary of Athena**, lies further east, about a ten-minute walk along the main road and on the opposite side. The most conspicuous building in the precinct is the **Tholos**, a fourth-century BC rotunda. Three of its dome-columns and their entablature have been re-constructed but while these amply demonstrate the original beauty of the building, its ultimate purpose still remains a mystery. The historic **Castalian spring** is located on a sharp bend between the Marmaria and the Sacred Precinct. It is marked by niches for votive offerings and by the remains of an archaic fountain house – water still flows from a cleft in the Phaedriades cliffs.

Modern Dhelfí, just west of the site, enjoys an impressive location. Almost entirely geared to tourism, its attraction lies in its mountain setting, its proximity to the ancient ruins and its access to the popular skiing centre of Mount Parnassós. There is a helpful tourist office (Mon–Fri 7.30am–2.30pm; ⊕226 50 82 900) in the town hall on the lower main thoroughfare.

Up to six **buses** a day run direct to Delphi from Athens, leaving from the Liossíon terminal. It's also possible to travel by train, though this involves changing at Livadhiá and a local bus from there. If you're driving, take the old road towards Thebes.

The Delphic Oracle

The origins of the Delphic Oracle are uncertain but it was believed by the ancients that the first oracle established on this spot was dedicated to Gea (Mother Earth) and to Poseidon (the Earth Shaker). Subsequently the serpent Python, son of Gea, was installed in a nearby cave, and communication made through the Pythian priestess. Python was later slain by Apollo, whose cult had been imported from Crete. Legend has it that he arrived in the form of a dolphin – hence the name *Delphoi*.

For over a thousand years thereafter, a steady stream of pilgrims made its way up the dangerous mountain paths to Delphi in order seek divine direction in matters of war, worship, love or business. On arrival they would sacrifice a sheep or a goat and, depending on the omens, wait to submit questions inscribed on lead tablets. The Pythian priestess, a simple and devout village woman of fifty or more years in age, would chant her prophecies from a tripod positioned over the oracular chasm.

Many of the oracular answers were equivocal. Croesus, for example, was told that if he embarked on war against neighbouring Persia he would destroy a mighty empire; he did – his own. But it's hard to imagine that the oracle would have retained its popularity and influence for so long without offering predominantly sound advice.

One theory suggests that the prophetic inspiration of the Oracle was due to geologic phenomena. The oracle may have been deliberately sited over a geological or earthquake fault line that emitted trance-inducing gases such as methane or ethane, which could have produced the kind of trances and behaviour described by ancient witnesses of the Pythian priestesses.

Aráhova

The strung-out village of Aráhova, dwarfed by the peaks of Parnassós, is a picturesque little place, with its vernacular architecture, stone walls, wooden eaves, and shops selling all kinds of craftware and foodstuffs. During the winter it's popular with skiers, but it's worth a brief stop at any time of year to browse the wide variety of local produce – including wine, cheese and local pasta known as *hilópittes* – and to wander the attractive backstreets winding off the busy main road. There's a wide selection of good places to wine and dine, many distinctly upmarket. Not all are open in summer, however.

▼ TEMPLE OF ZEUS, DELPHI

The local festival of Áyios Yeóryios (April 23, or the Tuesday after Easter if this date falls within Lent), centred on the church at the top of the hill, is the excuse for almost two days of continuous partying, and one of the best opportunities in the region to see authentic folk-dancing.

There are daily buses to and from Athens and Delphi.

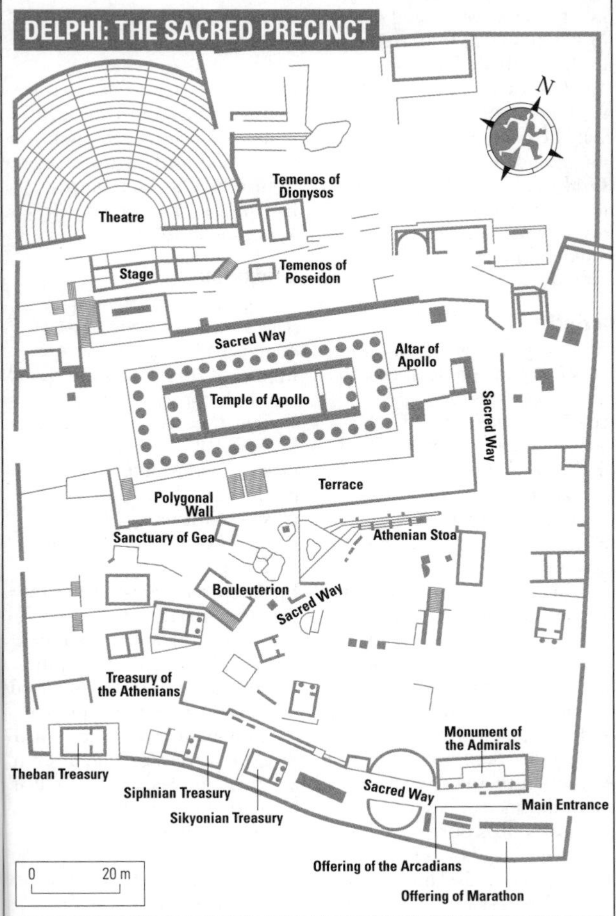

Mount Parnassós

Mount Parnassós, rising to almost 2500 metres at its highest point, is a popular climbing and walking destination, as well as a ski centre in winter. The heights are easily accessible, and though they no longer rank as complete wilderness, thanks to the ski station above Aráhova and its accompanying paraphernalia of lifts, snack bars and access roads, the area remains an attractive break from the city.

The best routes for walkers are those up from Dhelfi to the **Corycian cave** (practicable from April to Nov, but not in midsummer without a dawn start), or the ascent to the summit of **Mount Liákoura** (2455m) that commences from the Yerondóvrakhos ski station (May–Oct only). With your own transport you could drive up the mountain from Aráhova on the south, or from Lílea, Polýdhrosos or Amfília on the north slope, any of which can easily be combined with a walk. For extended explorations, Road Editions' 1:50,000 map no. 42, *Parnassos*, is a wise investment, with an attached booklet summarizing a route to the Corycian cave.

Corinth

Corinth daily: summer 8.30am–7pm; winter 8am–5pm. €6. Acrocorinth: summer daily 8am–7pm; winter Tues–Sun 8.30am–3pm. Free. The ruins of ancient Corinth, which displaced Athens as capital of the Greek province in Roman times, occupy a rambling sequence of sites that encompass sections of ancient walls, outlying stadiums, gymnasiums and necropolises. The main enclosure is given a sense of scale by the majestic ruin of the Temple of Apollo. Most compelling, though, are the ruins of the medieval city, which occupy the stunning acropolis of **Acrocorinth**, towering 565m above the ancient city on an enormous mass of rock, still largely encircled by two kilometres of wall. This became one of Greece's most powerful fortresses during the Middle Ages.

There's a four-kilometre climb to the entrance gate, but once you've reached the top and are overlooking the Saronic and Corinthian gulfs, you really get a sense of its strategic importance. Amid the extensive remains, you wander through a jumble of chapels, mosques, houses and battlements, erected in turn by Greeks, Romans, Byzantines, Frankish crusaders, Venetians and Turks.

▼ ACROCORINTH

Epidauros

Site: daily 8am–7pm. Museum: summer Mon noon–7pm, Tues–Sun 8am–7pm; winter closes 5pm. €6. Epidauros (Epídhavros) is visited primarily for its stunning ancient **theatre**, built around 330–320 BC, whose setting makes a compelling venue for productions of Classical drama as part of the annual Hellenic Festival (see p.170). With its backdrop of rolling hills, Epidauros's 14,000-seat theatre merges perfectly into the landscape – so well, in fact, that it was rediscovered only in the nineteenth century. Constructed with mathematical precision, it has near-perfect acoustics – such that you can hear coins, or even matches, dropped in the circular orchestra from the highest of the 54 tiers of seats.

The theatre, however, is just one component of what was one of the most important sanctuaries in the ancient world, dedicated to the healing god Asklepios. A place of pilgrimage for half a millennium, from the sixth century BC into Roman times, it's now a World Heritage site. Close by the theatre is a small museum, which is best visited before you explore the rest of the sanctuary – most of the ruins visible today are just foundations, so calling here helps identify some of the former buildings. The finds displayed show the progression

▲ EPIDAUROS

of medical skills and cures used at the **Asklepion**; there are tablets recording miraculous cures alongside advanced-looking surgical instruments.

Náfplio

A lively, beautifully sited town, Náfplio exudes a grand, slightly faded elegance, inherited from the days when it was the fledgling capital of modern Greece in the early nineteenth century. The postcard-pretty old town, with its paved and mostly pedestrianized streets, has an abundance of colourful and tastefully decorated restaurants and handicraft shops, and there's a pleasant buzz that you don't often witness in Greek towns. For the fit, the climb up to the twin fortresses of Palamídhi

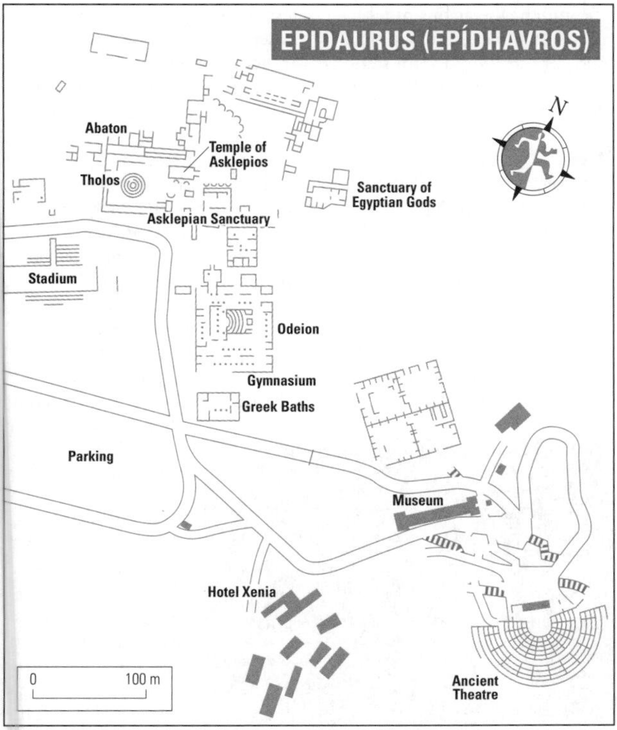

EPIDAURUS (EPÍDHAVROS)

N
Abaton
Temple of Asklepios
Tholos
Sanctuary of Egyptian Gods
Asklepian Sanctuary
Stadium
Odeion
Gymnasium
Greek Baths
Parking
Museum
Hotel Xenia
Ancient Theatre
0 100 m

(daily: summer 8am–7pm; winter 8am–6.30pm; €4), out on the headland and overlooking the old town, is well worth the effort. The town's third fort, the stunning Boúrtzi, occupies the Ayíou Theodhórou islet offshore from the harbour, and was built in 1473 by the Venetians to control the shipping lane to the town and to much of Árgos bay.

Café life – swelled at weekends by crowds of visiting Athenians – reaches the heights of urban chic in the well-patronized cafés lining the palm-tree fringed western seafront of Bouboulínas. Things are quieter on Platía Syndágmatos, where places stay open late.

You can get to Náfplio by bus or – much slower but much more attractive – by twice-daily train. Both bus and train stations are within a 500m walk of the old town precinct.

Tiryns

Daily: summer 8am–7pm; winter 8.30am–3pm. €3. In Mycenaean times the ancient fortress of Tiryns (Tíryntha) commanded the coastal approaches to Árgos and Mycenae. The Aegean shore, however, gradually receded, leaving this impressive structure stranded on a low hillock in today's plains, surrounded by citrus groves, alongside a large modern prison. The setting is less impressive than that of its showy neighbour Mycenae, which in part explains why this highly accessible, substantial site is relatively empty of visitors; the opportunity to wander about Homer's "wall-girt Tiryns" in near-solitude is worth taking. The site lies just to the east of the main Árgos–Náfplio road, and frequent local buses drop off and pick up passengers outside.

Mycenae

Tucked into a fold of the hills just east of the road from Kórinthos to Árgos, the **citadel** at Mycenae (Mykínes) (daily: summer 8am–7pm; winter 8.30am–3pm; €6) bears testament above all to the obsession of the German archeologist Heinrich Schliemann (who also excavated the site of Troy) with proving that the tales of Homer had their basis in fact.

The extensive site is made up of two parts – the citadel itself and the Treasury of Atreus. The most visually arresting part of the citadel is the Lion Gate, whose huge sloping gateposts and walls were considered Cyclopean by later Greeks, who could only imagine that a Cyclops could have constructed them. Beyond the Lion Gate is an impressive Grave Circle known as "A" and originally thought by Schliemann to be the actual tomb of Agamemnon. It was here that the famous gold death mask (see p.10) was found in 1876. The

▲ TIRYNS

▲ MYCENAE

rest of the site is scattered over the hillside, while just down the road is the tremendously impressive **Treasury of Atreus**, which is what is now described as the **Tomb of Agamemnon**. This was certainly a royal burial vault at a late stage in Mycenae's history, so the attribution to Agamemnon or his father is as good as any. Whoever it might have belonged to, this beehive-like structure is an impressive monument to Mycenaean building skills.

Égina

Barely an hour and a half from Pireás, the rural island of Égina can easily be visited in a day. Most visitors spend their day ambling around the boat-packed waterfront or through the back streets of the island's main town – also called Égina. Making use of the decent local bus service, you could also head for the exceptionally well-preserved, beautiful fifth-century BC **Temple of Afaia** (Mon–Fri 8.15am–7pm daily; €4), which

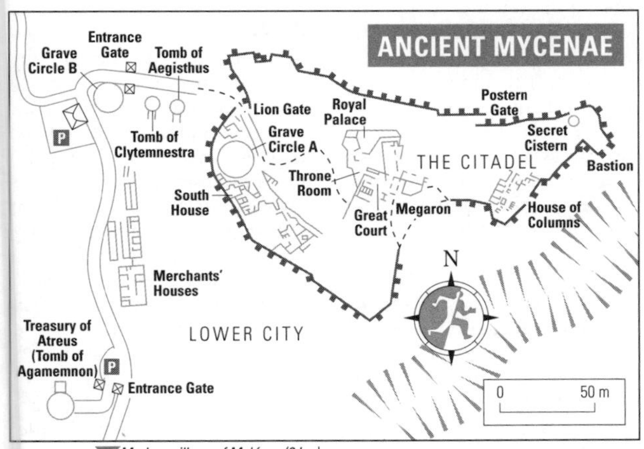

▲ FERRY TICKET BOOTHS

stands in lonely vigil at the northeastern corner of the island; or the low-key fishing village of Pérdhika with its cosy harbour and fish tavernas that are often frequented by Athenian yachties; or perhaps the east coast resort village of Ayía Marína.

There's a good selection of accommodation in the port of Égina, and plenty of good tavernas – restaurants here tend to specialize in fish, usually rather cheaper than in Athens or Pireás. The island is also a big producer of pistachio nuts, and during the summer months you can see the orchards around the island laden with them.

Transport to and from the island is frequent and good; you've a choice of ferries or hydrofoils, and advance booking is unnecessary – just turn up at the ferry quay in Pireás and buy a ticket from the booths.

Angístri

Just one hour's ferry trip from Pireás – or fifteen minutes from Égina – Angístri is small enough to be explored on foot, from the port of Skála to the delightful little bay, beach and hamlet of Apónisos, with its two tiny offshore islets. On the way you'll pass Mýlos (Megalokhóri) and the small farming community of Limenária, set at the edge of a fertile plateau in the southeast corner of the island.

There's a decent sandy beach at Skála, though you may find a little more seclusion at Halikádha pebble beach (clothing optional), backed by crumbling cliffs and pine-covered hills on the east side of the island.

Póros

Separated from the mainland by just a 450-metre strait, Póros (The Ford) is in fact two islands: Sferiá (occupied almost entirely by Póros Town), and the much more extensive Kalávria. Its proximity to Pireás means it's hugely popular, making Póros Town, which is exceptionally picturesque, a lively, animated place to be. The cafés, waterfront tavernas and restaurants entertain a seemingly endless flow of customers, while fishermen attempt to sell their catch to passers by. There's little specific to seek out, although the hilltop clocktower and small, well-labelled archeological museum (Mon–Sat 8.30am–3pm; free) are worth a look. For a more peaceful escape, head over to Kalávria, whose south coast is fringed by a succession of pine-shaded bays.

Ídhra

The port and town of Ídhra (Hydra), with tiers of greystone mansions and white-walled, red-tiled houses climbing steeply up from a perfect horseshoe harbour, make a magnificent spectacle. Both beautiful and peaceful – thanks to an almost total ban on motor vehicles – it is not surprisingly popular. You'll see it at its best if you visit on a weekday or out of season: on the plus side, the visitors mean plenty of excellent restaurants and cafés, getting less expensive as you head away from the waterfront.

The mansions themselves, most of them built during the eighteenth century on the accumulated wealth of a remarkable merchant fleet, were designed by Venetian and Genoese architects and are still the great monuments of the island. A town map is available if you are interested in seeking any out – some are labelled at the entrance with "*Oikía*" (home) and the family name.

Ídhra also reputedly has no fewer than 365 churches – a total claimed by many a Greek island, but here with some justice. The most important is the church of Panayía Mitropóleos, with a distinctive clocktower and a Byzantine museum (Tues–Sun 10am–5pm; €2). Thanks to the lack of transport, few people venture away from the town, so a short walk will take you to surprising isolation; there are no real sandy beaches, but numerous rocky coves are accessible (with less effort, you can also get to many by boat or water-taxi from the harbour).

▲ POROS HARBOUR

Restaurants

Agora

Behind Égina Town's fish market on Panayioti Irioti 28, Égina ☎229 70 27 308. *Agora* is particularly good for relatively inexpensive seafood, and there's outdoor seating on the cobbles in summer.

Ta Alonia

At the junction for the Mount Parnassos ski centre, Aráhova ☎226 70 32 644. Popular haunt serving excellent *pittes* and good, solid mountain fare.

Andonis

Pérdhika, 9km from Égina Town, Égina ☎229 70 61 443. The most popular of the fish tavernas on the harbour here. A little pricey, but the high-quality dishes are still good value

En Etei 1929

Cnr Khr. Smýrnis & Markopoúlou, Náfplio ☎275 20 29 007. A shade upmarket, but worth it. The cuisine is European with Swiss overtones – fondue is on the menu – and pasta is a good choice.

Epikouros

Pavlou & Fredirikis 33, Dhelfí ☎226 50 83 250. One of the best eateries in Delphi, the wild boar stew is particularly good here – and the view from the terrace is stunning.

Kakanarakis

Vasilíssis Ólgas 18, Náfplio ☎275 20 25 371. Eves only. Lively place serving a variety of reasonably priced and dependably good *mezédhes*, plus dishes such as braised cockerel with noodles, and *kokkinistó* (meat simmered in tomato sauce).

Karathanasis

Aráhova ☎226 70 31 360. Filling soups in the cooler months, alongside draft wine and assorted meat dishes year round and roof-terrace seating in summer.

Karavolos

Póros ☎229 80 26 158. Eves only. Busy taverna serving *karavólos* (snails) and other imaginative fare such as *saganáki* (small skillet) dishes. It's signposted from the western waterfront.

Taverna Leonides

Epidauros ☎275 20 22 115. A friendly spot with a garden out back; book ahead if your visit coincides with a performance at the ancient theatre. Actors eat here after shows – photos on the wall testify to the patronage of Melina Mercouri, the Papandreous, François Mitterrand and Sir Peter Hall.

Mandraki

Skala, Angístri. Moderately priced unfussy grills and home cooking.

Moita

Ídhra ☎229 80 52 020. Just inland from the waterfront, *Moita* serves interesting seafood and Mediterranean fusion dishes. For that special evening it's worth splashing out.

Mykinaiko

Mykínes, Mycenae ☎275 10 76 724. One of the best in the village in terms of both quality and value, with excellent oven-cooked dishes and a robust draft red wine known as "Blood of Hercules" to wash it down.

O Naftis

Douzína 66, Póros ☎229 80 23 096. Popular with the yachting set, *Naftis* has a varied menu of grills, fish and *mezedes* as well as a relaxing location.

Oasis

Póros ☎229 80 22 955. One of the longer-established harbourside tavernas on Póros, the moderately expensive *Oasis* has a regular and faithful clientele – a good indication of its commitment to quality cooking.

Panagiota

Aráhova ☎226 70 32 735. A friendly, family-style taverna high above Aráhova, with fine, good-value lamb dishes, home-baked bread and rich chicken soup.

Taverna Parnassos

Metókhi, Angístri. It's worth the walk up the hill for the views and the good food here. Dine on *mayireftá* and enjoy the relaxing view down towards Skála.

Platanos

Póros ☎229 80 24 249. High up overlooking Póros port from a little square hosting a clutch of less obvious tavernas, *Platanos* specializes in meat dishes, and you can dine in the shade of a large plane tree.

To Steki

Panayioti Irioti 34, Égina ☎229 70 23 910. A small *mezédhes* place behind Égina Town's fish market, with inexpensive to moderate prices. The grilled octopus is particularly good.

I Taverna tou Stelara

Bouboulínas 73, Náfplio ☎275 20 28 818. A good spot for home-cooked *ladherá* (olive-oil-based dishes) and the fried calamari is also well done.

Vasilis

Staïkopoúlou 20–24, Náfplio ☎275 20 25 334. In a street where most of the establishments serve similar menus, *Vasilis* stands out through the freshness of its ingredients. Very reasonably priced, too.

Vakchos

Apollonos 31, Dhelfí ☎226 50 83 250. One of the better quality establishments in a village not particularly well known for great eateries. The view from this family place is quite stunning, and the food is good-quality traditional fare that's reasonable value for your euros.

Xeri Elia

Ídhra ☎229 80 52 886. A cosy and relatively inexpensive fish taverna in an old stone house that puts an inventive twist on filling *mayireftá* dishes.

Yambeia

Aráhova ☎226 70 32 730. Moderate-value bar-restaurant on the main street of Aráhova, operating as a café during the morning. The dishes are Italian-influenced dishes, and there's a small wine list, attentive service and pleasant ambience.

Yeitoniko

Ídhra ☎229 80 53 615. This popular taverna, about 500m inland from the port, has tables on its roof and a small veranda. Serves great home cooking and the pasta and vegetarian dishes are excellent value.

Accommodation

Accommodation

Hotels

Prices for accommodation are highly seasonal and in the lead-up to the Olympics well over half the city's hotels seemed to have been refurbished, raising their rates accordingly. The prices quoted in this guide represent the hotel's cheapest double room in high season; much of the year, you'll find rates are lower than this. By law, every room has to display its official rates on the back of the door: it is illegal for a hotelier to charge more than this, and you can normally expect to pay less. Most places have triple and even four-bed rooms, which can be a significant saving for a family or group.

Breakfast is included in the price at the more expensive hotels and is almost always available at extra cost if it's not included; check what you'll get, however, as the standard Greek hotel breakfast of a cup of weak coffee accompanied by a piece of dry cake and some jam is rarely worth paying for. Most of our recommendations will offer more than that – usually some form of bufffet.

The quarters of **Pláka**, **Monastiráki** and **Sýndagma** are atmospheric and within easy walking distance of all the main sites; hotels here are also relatively expensive, however, and may be noisy. Formerly gritty and sleazy but rapidly being gentrified, Omónia's **bazaar area** is the city at its most colourful, while nearby **Thissío** is rather smarter and airier. For more night-time peace, and better value, though, there's a lot to be said for heading for one of the quieter neighbourhoods a little further out. **Koukáki** and **Pangráti** are attractive parts of the city, and though slightly out of the way – twenty minutes' walk from Sýndagma or the heart of Pláka – compensate with excellent neighbourhood tavernas and cafés. Around **Exárhia** and **Platía Viktorías**, to the north of Omónia, you are again out of the tourist mainstream, but benefit from good-value local restaurants and the proximity of cinemas, clubs and bars.

Pláka

Acropolis House **Kódhrou 6 ⓣ210 32 22 344, ⓕ210 32 44 143. Metro Sýndagma.** A very clean, well-sited 150-year-old mansion much favoured by students and academics, who return year after year. Furnishings are eclectic and some rooms have private baths across the hall. Rates include breakfast. €60.

Booking accommodation

Athens hotels can be packed in midsummer, especially August – yet for most of the year there are enough beds in the city to go around, and to suit most wallets and tastes. It makes sense to **book in advance** if possible, or to find a phone and ring around on arrival, rather than walk the streets looking: almost every hotel and hostel will have an English-speaking receptionist.

The best rates may well be offered on the **Internet** – type "Athens hotels" into any search engine and you'll come up with dozens of hotel search sites, often with excellent-value special offers. If you do just set out and do the rounds, try to start as early as possible in the day. Especially in the cheaper hotels, standards can vary greatly between rooms, so try to see alternatives before you check in.

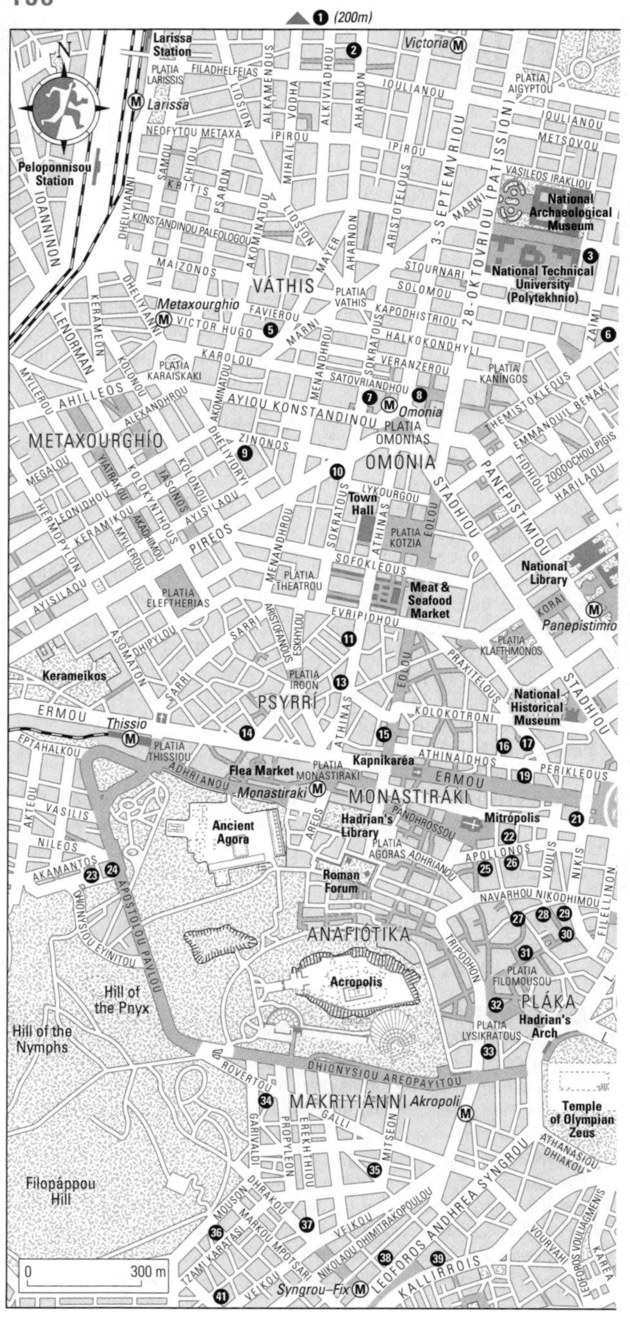
1 (200m)
Larissa Station
Victoria
Larissa
Peloponnisou Station
National Archaeological Museum
National Technical University (Polytekhnio)
VÁTHIS
PLATIA VATHIS
Metaxourghio
PLATIA KARAISKAKI
METAXOURGHÍO
Omonia
PLATIA OMONIAS
OMÓNIA
Town Hall
PLATIA KOTZIA
PLATIA THEATROU
PLATIA ELEFTHERIAS
Meat & Seafood Market
National Library
Panepistimio
PLATIA KLAFTHMONOS
Kerameikos
PLATIA IROON
PSYRRÍ
National Historical Museum
Thissio
PLATIA THISSIOU
Kapnikaréa
Flea Market
PLATIA MONASTIRAKI
Monastiraki
MONASTIRÁKI
Mitrópolis
Ancient Agora
Hadrian's Library
PLATIA AGORAS
Roman Forum
ANAFIÓTIKA
Acropolis
PLATIA FILOMOUSOU
PLÁKA
Hadrian's Arch
PLATIA LYSIKRATOUS
Hill of the Pnyx
Hill of the Nymphs
MAKRIYIÁNNI
Akropoli
Temple of Olympian Zeus
Filopáppou Hill
Syngrou-Fix
0 300 m

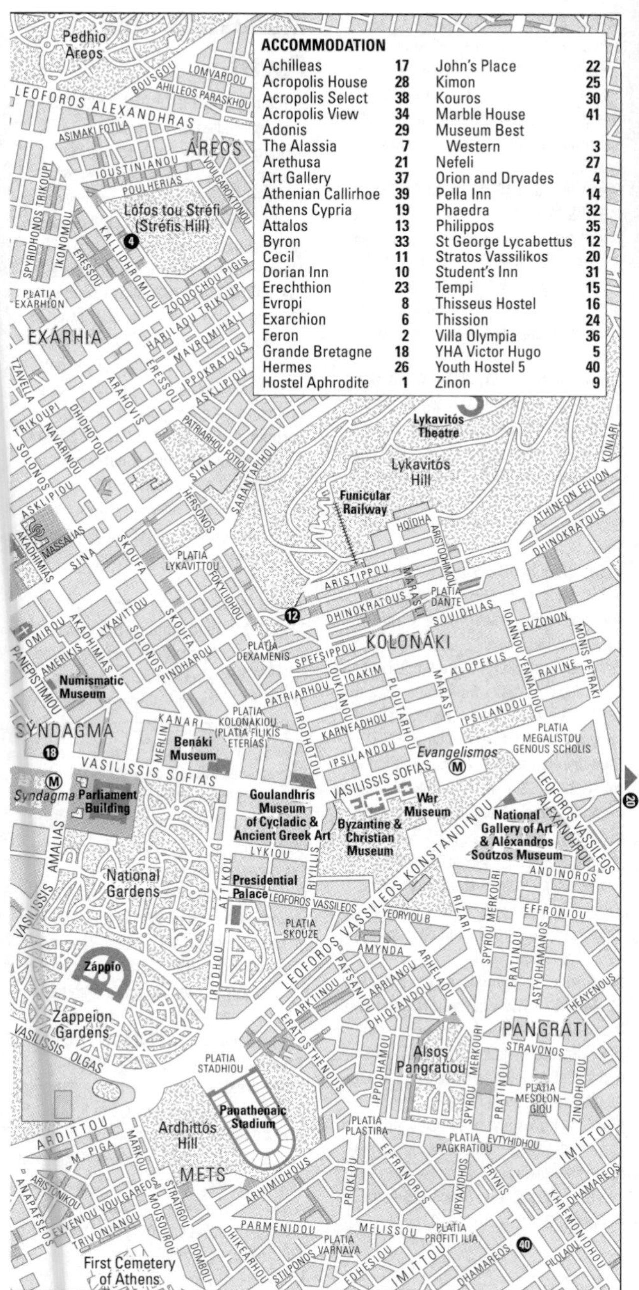
ACCOMMODATION
Achilleas 17
Acropolis House 28
Acropolis Select 38
Acropolis View 34
Adonis 29
The Alassia 7
Arethusa 21
Art Gallery 37
Athenian Callirhoe 39
Athens Cypria 19
Attalos 13
Byron 33
Cecil 11
Dorian Inn 10
Erechthion 23
Evropi 8
Exarchion 6
Feron 2
Grande Bretagne 18
Hermes 26
Hostel Aphrodite 1
John's Place 22
Kimon 25
Kouros 30
Marble House 41
Museum Best Western 3
Nefeli 27
Orion and Dryades 4
Pella Inn 14
Phaedra 32
Philippos 35
St George Lycabettus 12
Stratos Vassilikos 20
Student's Inn 31
Tempi 15
Thisseus Hostel 16
Thission 24
Villa Olympia 36
YHA Victor Hugo 5
Youth Hostel 5 40
Zinon 9
Pedhio Areos
ÁREOS
Lófos tou Stréfi (Stréfis Hill)
EXÁRHIA
Lykavitós Theatre
Lykavitós Hill
Funicular Railway
KOLONÁKI
Numismatic Museum
SÝNDAGMA
Benáki Museum
Evangelismos
Syndagma
Parliament Building
Goulandhrís Museum of Cycladic & Ancient Greek Art
Byzantine & Christian Museum
War Museum
National Gallery of Art & Aléxandros Soútzos Museum
National Gardens
Presidential Palace
Záppio
Zappeíon Gardens
PANGRÁTI
Alsos Pangratiou
Panathenaic Stadium
Ardhittós Hill
METS
First Cemetery of Athens

Adonis **Kódhrou 3 ⓣ210 32 49 737, ⓕ210 32 31 602. Metro Sýndagma.** A modern, low-rise *pension* across the street from *Acropolis House*, with some suites. The rooftop café has a stunning view of the Acropolis and central Athens; breakfast included. €60.

Byron **Výronos 19 ⓣ210 32 53 554, ⓕ210 32 20 276. Metro Akrópoli.** Set on a quiet side street within walking distance of the Acropolis and Pláka museums, the *Byron* is a fairly basic place, attractively renovated with a/c and TV in each room. A few upper rooms have impressive Acropolis views. €80.

Kouros **Kódhrou 11, Pláka ⓣ210 32 27 431. Metro Sýndagma.** A slightly faded atmospheric *pension*, but with adequate facilities: shared baths and sinks in rooms. Doubles are overpriced but singles are better value. Some balconies overlook the pedestrianized street, the continuation of Voulís. €60.

Nefeli **Iperídhou 16 ⓣ210 32 28 044, ⓕ210 32 25 800. Metro Sýndagma.** The entrance of this modern-looking hotel is actually at Hatzimiháli 2. Comfortably faded rooms all come with TV and a/c, though the lower floors do suffer from some noise at night and service can be mixed. Discount for stays of more than two days. €80.

Phaedra **Herefóndos 16, cnr Adhrianoú ⓣ210 32 27 795, ⓕ210 32 38 461. Metro Akrópoli.** Simple, newly renovated place that's one of the best deals in Pláka. Quiet at night, thanks to its location at the junction of two pedestrian streets, with polite, welcoming management. The cheaper rooms share bathrooms but all rooms have TV and a/c. €50.

Student's Inn **Kydhathinéon 16 ⓣ210 32 44 808, ⓦwww.studenttravellersinn.com. Metro Akrópoli.** This long-established travellers' haunt is a mixture of hotel and hostel, recently renovated and painted. All rooms have en-suite baths, and there are some triples and quadruples, as well as dorm beds. Not the quietest location, but nice otherwise, with a small courtyard and Internet facilities open to non-residents. Dorms €22–25, rooms €60.

Monastiráki and Psyrrí

Achilleas **Lékka 21 ⓣ210 32 33 197, ⓦwww.achilleashotel.gr. Metro Sýndagma.** Three-star hotel in a central location on a relatively quiet street. All rooms have been renovated and have a/c and TV. Breakfast is served on the roof terrace, weather permitting. €140.

Athens Cypria **Dhiomías 5 ⓣ210 32 38 034, ⓕ210 32 48 792. Metro Sýndagma.** Standard, modern tourist hotel, but with all the luxuries – a/c, satellite TV, mini-bar, data ports – and good value for what you get. Very close to Sýndagma. The more expensive rooms have Acropolis views. €100.

Hermes **Apóllonos 19 ⓣ210 32 35 514, ⓔinfohermes@accommodate.gr. Metro Sýndagma.** Conveniently located two-star hotel, with comfortable, well-equipped, newly decorated rooms, and a hearty buffet breakfast included in the rather inflated price. €120.

John's Place **Patróöu 5 ⓣ210 32 29 719. Metro Sýndagma.** In a peaceful backstreet of Mitrópoleos, this basic hotel has rather dark rooms and shared bathrooms. It's clean and inexpensive however, and there's a cheap restaurant on the ground floor. €40.

Kimon **Apóllonos 27 ⓣ & ⓕ210 33 14 658. Metro Sýndagma.** A simple place, but the recently upgraded rooms here are spotlessly clean with TV and a/c. A few of the upper rooms have stunning Acropolis views. €60.

Pella Inn **Ermoú 104 ⓣ210 32 50 598, ⓦwww.pella-inn.gr. Metro Thissío.** One of the best deals in the area, this family-run hotel has enthusiastic management and startling views of the Acropolis from the third floor up. €95.

Tempi **Eólou 29 ⓣ210 32 13 175, ⓔtempihotel@travelling.gr. Metro Monastiráki.** A favourite with students and budget travellers. The rooms are tiny, most have shared facilities, and hot water can be sparse. But the view of the flower market at Ayía Iríni across the quiet pedestrian walkway is enchanting, and it's within walking distance of most central sights. There's also a book exchange, drinks, fridge, plus a handy affiliated travel agency. €55.

Thisseus Hostel Thisséos 10 ⓣ210 32 45 960. Metro Sýndagma. You don't get much more central than this – three blocks west of Sýndagma – nor much cheaper. No frills, but clean enough, and with a kitchen for guests' use, and some three- and four-bed dorms. €30.

Thissío, Gázi and Áno Petrálona

Erechthion Flammaríou 8 ⓣ210 34 59 606, ⓕ210 34 62 756. Metro Thissío. A reasonable mid-range option in this lively area behind the Acropolis. All rooms have a/c and TV. €95.

Thission Apostólou Pávlou 25 ⓣ210 34 67 634, ⓕ210 34 62 756. Metro Thissío. Somewhat better value than the nearby *Erechthion*, this friendly place has a/c and TV in all rooms, and fine views from the roof terrace. €100.

Platía Omonías and around

Attalos Athinás 29 ⓣ210 32 12 801, ⓦwww.attalos.gr. Metro Monastiráki. Modern hotel with clean, comfortable rooms with a/c and TV, friendly management and great Acropolis views from the rooftop bar. €80.

The Alassia Sokrátous 50, Omónia ⓣ210 52 74 000, ⓦwww.thealassia.com.gr. Metro Omónia. Renovated in 2002, the Alassia is a pleasant find in what is still a rather undeveloped accommodation area. Its designer decor is apparent as soon as you enter the lobby. Rooms are on the small side, but are elegant and well sound-insulated. Good value for money. €120.

Hostel Aphrodite Inárdhou 12, cnr Mikhaïl Vódha 65 ⓣ210 88 39 249, ⓦwww.hostelaphrodite.com. Metro Viktorías. Under the same management as the *Student's Inn* in Pláka, and a very similar set-up. Friendly and clean, with a/c and hot water in shared bathrooms, safe, free baggage storage and Internet access. Dorms €17, bed in two-bed dorm €23, rooms €40.

Cecil Athinás 39 ⓣ210 32 17 079, ⓦwww.cecil.gr. Metro Monastiráki. Loving restoration of a run-down *pension* has re-created the charm of the 150-year-old mansion; attractively decorated rooms are larger than average and all have a/c. The location in the heart of the market district, gracious management, roof garden and hearty breakfast with Cretan jams and yogurt make this a delight. €95.

Dorian Inn Pireós 15-17, Omónia ⓣ210 523 9782, ⓦwww.greekhotel.com/athens/dorianinn. Metro Omónia. Very close to Platía Omonías and handy for the Acropolis, this is a bustling hotel popular with both business visitors and tourists. The rooftop garden boasts a pool and excellent views. €160.

Evropi Satovriándhou 7 ⓣ210 52 23 081. Metro Omónia. Very basic old-fashioned hotel with spacious rooms, made even cooler by ceiling fans. Best-value singles in town and reasonably quiet, despite being only a block from Platía Omonías. €35.

Feron Férron 43, Platía Viktorías ⓣ210 82 32 083. Metro Viktorías. A small, simple hotel with cheerful staff and en-suite baths in all rooms. Very good value. €80.

Zinon Keramikoú 3 and Zínonos ⓣ210 52 45 711, ⓦwww.bestwestern.com. Metro Omónia. A comfortable, reasonably priced, three-star Best Western hotel just off Platía Omonías. Good-sized rooms have been recently renovated, and come with satellite TV and a complimentary bottle of wine. €95.

Exárhia and Neápoli

Exarchion Themistokléous 55, Platía Exárhia ⓣ210 38 01 256, ⓕ210 38 03 296. Metro Omónia. Big 1960s high-rise hotel, with an excellent location right on the square – though this means the rooms on the lower floors can be noisy. €100.

Museum Best Western Bouboulínas 16 ⓣ210 38 05 611, ⓦwww.bestwestern.com. Metro Omónia. Recently taken over by the Best Western group and upgraded to its international standards, this nicely placed hotel is at the end of the green strip separating the National Archeological Museum and the Polytekhnío. €110.

Orion and Dryades **Anexartisías 5 ⓣ210 36 27 362, ⓔorion-dryades@mail.com. Metro Omónia.** Quiet, well-run twin hotels across from the Lófos Stréfi park – a steep uphill walk. Reception is in the cheaper *Orion*, which has shared bathrooms, a kitchen, and communal area on the roof with an amazing view of central Athens. All rooms in the *Dryades* are en suite with a/c and TV. €110.

Kolonáki & Lykavitós Hill

St George Lycabettus **Kleoménous 2, Kolonáki ⓣ210 729 0711, ⓦwww.sglycabettus.gr. Metro Evangelismós.** One of the classic five-star hotels in Athens, the St George has one of the best locations, high up on Lykavitos hill overlooking Sýndagma and the Acropolis. Tasetfully done up in boutique-hotel style, there's abundant marble and leather in the public areas plus a welcome rooftop pool. €145 for courtyard view, €220 looking out on the Acropolis.

Stratos Vassilikos **Michalakópoulou 114, Ilísia ⓣ210 77 06 611, ⓦwww.airotel.gr. Metro Mégaro Moussikís.** Predominantly a business hotel, but very comfortable, newly renovated and with all the facilities you'd expect, including TV and Internet in the rooms, marble bathrooms, and even a tiny gym. Good metro and bus connections from its location near the US embassy. €170.

Sýndagma and around

Arethusa **Mitropóleos 6–8 and Níkis 12 ⓣ210 32 29 431, ⓔarethusa@travelling.gr. Metro Sýndagma.** This modern, quiet hotel with a/c and TV in each room caters to independent travellers and small groups. The reception staff are helpful and enthusiastic, and rates quite reasonable considering the excellent location. €120.

Grande Bretagne **Vasiléos Yioryíou 1, Platía Sýndagma ⓣ210 33 30 000, ⓦwww.grandebretagne.gr.** If someone else is paying, try to get them to put you up at the *Grande Bretagne*, the grandest of all Athens' hotels with the finest location in town. Recently refurbished, it really is magnificent, with every conceivable facility. Treatments in the spa cost more than a night at most hotels – rooms are over €300 even for an off-season special offer. €400.

Mets, Pangráti and Koukáki

Acropolis Select **Falírou 37–39 ⓣ210 92 11 611, ⓦwww.acropoliselect.gr. Metro Syngroú-Fix.** An excellent, tastefully renovated boutique hotel within ten minutes' walk of the Acropolis. Pastel and earthy shades characterize the welcoming rooms, which have individually controlled a/c, satellite TV and modem ports. €125.

Acropolis View **Webster 10, Koukáki ⓣ210 92 17 303, ⓦwww.acropolisview.gr. Metro Akrópoli.** A well-maintained small hotel on a quiet residential street whose front rooms with balconies and roof garden live up to its name. All rooms have a/c, TV and fridge, an ample breakfast is included and the lobby sports a friendly bar. €130.

Art Gallery **Erekhthíou 5, Koukáki ⓣ210 92 38 376, ⓔcotes@otenet.gr. Metro Syngroú-Fix.** A mansion that was formerly the home of a member of the owner's family, this popular *pension* is named for the original artworks on the walls. Rooms are plain, but the place is distinguished by knowledgeable and helpful staff, a convenient location just a short walk from the metro, and a bountiful breakfast (at extra cost) served on a sunny terrace with Acropolis view. €70.

Athenian Callirhoe **Kalliróis 32, cnr Petmeza ⓣ210 92 15 353, ⓦwww.tac.gr. Metro Syngroú-Fix.** Situated between Koukáki and the centre, the *Callirhoe* was made over a couple of years back as an upmarket "designer" hotel. It's already starting to look slightly faded, but is centrally located and has good facilities – including TV and Internet in the rooms and a small gym – making it popular with business and leisure travellers alike. Worth checking for offers. €180.

Marble House Cul-de-sac off A. Zínni 35A, Koukáki ⊕210 92 34 058, ©info@marblehouse.gr. Metro Syngroú-Fix. Easily the best value in Koukáki, with a very helpful management. It's often full, so call ahead. Eight of the rooms have a/c (for extra charge); most rooms have a bath, and there are also two self-catering studios for longer stays. €45.

Philippos Mitséon 3, Makryiánni ⊕210 922 36111, ⊛www.philipposhotel.gr. Metro Akrópoli. A small yet comfortable modern hotel located conveniently on the southeast side of the Acropolis. There's a large atrium for breakfast or afternoon coffee. €195.

Villa Olympia Karatzá 6, Koukáki ⊕210 92 37 650. Officially designated for long stays only, the rudimentary no-frills rooms are often available to tourists on a daily basis in this ramshackle old house, run by an Englishwoman. Basic, but by far the cheapest place in town. €20.

Suburban Athens

Acropole Goúnari 7, Pireás ⊕210 41 73 313, ⊛www.acropole-hotel.gr. See map on p.127. Perhaps the pick of the hotels in the Pireás port area, this newly renovated place has a variety of rooms including triples; some with Jacuzzi. Breakfast room and bar downstairs. €60.

Astir Palace Vouliagmeni Apollónos 40, Vouliagméni ⊕210 89 02 000, ⊛www.astir.gr. The *Astir Palace* resort complex occupies some 75 acres of a private pine-covered peninsula, 25km from downtown. It has three hotels and villas, with pools, private beaches, water sports, tennis courts, a health club and no fewer than six restaurants. A shuttle bus runs twice daily to central Athens (in case the weather prevents you using the helipad) and there's every other conceivable facility including a major thalassotherapy spa. From €220.

Delfini Leohárous 7, Pireás ⊕210 41 73 110, ⊛www.4peiraias.gr/delfini. See map on p.127. If you have a late ferry arrival or early departure and want a functional, convenient hotel, this is it. Tiny rooms, but each is nicely done out with fridge and balcony; there are also some multi-bed rooms available. €50, but discounts if you show this book.

Kefalari Suites Pendélis 1, Kifissiá ⊕210 62 33 333, ⊛www.kefalarisuites.gr. See map on p.126. A dozen extremely luxurious suites, each with its own decorative theme and with every facility you might want. A very long way from the bustle of central Athens. €200–500.

Mistral Vasiléos Pávlou 105, Kastella, Pireás ⊕210 41 17 150, ⊛www.mistral.gr. See map on p.127. Upscale, rather bland hotel, but undeniably comfortable and with fine sea views, looking out over Mikrolímano. Satellite TV, data ports and many other facilities in the rooms. Much better value than similar quality places in the centre. €110.

Hostels

There are only a couple of places in Athens that can strictly be described as hostels, and only one of these is officially recognized. Several of the cheaper hotels listed above, however, offer beds in shared rooms. We've specified where this is the case – they're significantly more expensive than these hostels, but generally more centrally located.

YHA Victor Hugo 16 ⓣ210 52 34 170, ⓕ210 52 34 015. Metro Metaxourghío.
Between the train stations and Omónia, the only official youth hostel in Athens is friendly, informative and, although a little frayed at the edges, includes a café and left-luggage store. Annual membership costs €15; if you're not a member €2.50 per day is added to the cost of a bed. Dorms €8.

Youth Hostel #5 Damaréos 75, Pangráti, near the huge Profítis Ilías church ⓣ210 75 19 530, ⓔy-hostels@otenet.gr.
A bit out of the way, but this private hostel behind a green door is located in a quiet neighbourhood, is very friendly, and has no curfew. Trolleys #2 and #11 pass nearby. Dorms €9.

Campsites

The city's **campsites** are out in the suburbs and not especially cheap – they're only really worth using if you have a camper van to park. Phone ahead in season to book space.

Athens Camping Leofóros Athinón 198–200 ⓣ210 58 14 114.
The closest campsite to the centre of Athens, re-opened after a revamp. Facilities include a minimarket, snack-bar and plenty of hot water. Take the Elefsína bus #A16 from Platía Eleftherias.

Camping Nea Kifissia ⓣ210 80 75 579.
Located in the cool, leafy suburb of Néa Kifissiá, with a very welcome swimming pool. Take bus #A7 from Platía Káningos or metro to Kifissiá and transfer onto bus #528 to the stop close to the campsite.

Várkiza Camping ⓣ210 89 73 614.
Beachfront location just off the main road, some 20km south of the centre, with a swimming pool, bar and restaurant. Bus #A3 or #E2 from Amalías to Glyfádha then #115 or #116 to Várkiza.

Essentials

Essentials

Arrival

A new airport and substantial investment in transport links have transformed arriving in Athens. The airport is linked to the city by bus, metro and a fast expressway, while plenty of taxis and city buses service Pireás for those arriving by boat. Even driving in is relatively straightforward thanks to the new expressways.

By air

Athens' modernistic **Eleftherios Venizelos airport** (Ⓦwww.aia.gr) lies some 26km east of the city. Facilities are excellent, with ample money-changing bureaux, two American Express offices and several ATMs. Luggage-storage facilities are open round the clock, as are the shops, newsstands, cafés, a food court and fast-food restaurants. There's also an official **EOT** tourist office (daily 8am–10pm; ⓣ210 35 45 101). It's worth calling in here to pick up their excellent map, and up-to-date information on museum and site opening hours.

Public transport from the airport is in a state of flux, so it's worth picking up the latest leaflet on the situation, widely available at the airport. From summer 2004, **metro** line 3 should extend to Dhoukíssis Plakentías station, from where metro trains will share the suburban rail lines to the airport. With around four trains an hour, this should be the most convenient way into the centre. Alternatively, **express bus** #E95 (approx every 20min midnight–7am, every 30min 7am–7pm, every 15min 7pm–midnight; 70min) runs to Sýndagma Square in the centre of town via Ethnikí Ámyna metro station; #E94 (every 10min 7am–7pm, less frequently till midnight) goes to Ethnikí Ámyna only. The journey is quicker if you change to the metro at Ethnikí Ámyna, but this is not easy if you've got a lot of luggage. Again, bus routes may change as a result of the extension of the metro. Others are #E96 (every 20min 7am–9pm, every 40min 9pm–7am) to Pireás via the coastal suburbs of Voúla and Glyfádha; the #E92 (roughly every 45min 9am–9pm, every 90min 10.30pm–8am) to the northern suburb of Kifissiá; #E93 (roughly every 35min 6am–midinght, hourly midnight–6am) to Kifisós intercity bus station; and #E97 (every 45–50min 6am–6pm, every 60min 7pm–5am) to Dháfni metro station. All these services cost €2.90, and the **ticket** (an *imerísio*) is valid on all Athens public transport for 24 hours. They should be bought from a booth beside the stops, or, if this is closed, can be purchased on the bus: make sure you have small change. You need to validate the ticket once on the airport bus, and again for your first trip on the metro or city bus. When departing, it's worth buying your ticket, available from any city metro station, 24 hours in advance, to have a day's free use of the transport system as well as your journey to the airport.

Getting into Athens by **taxi** is also pretty swift. You can get to the city centre via the Attikí Odhós Expressway and the Ymittós Ring Road in less than thirty minutes at slow traffic times and in under an hour at peak times. The Attikí Odhós Expressway also links the airport with a large swathe of northern Athens and runs right around the city as far as Elefsína. A taxi **fare** is roughly €12–15 to central Athens or Pireás. Before setting out in a taxi, make sure that the meter is switched on to the correct rate (see taxis, p.167), but note that there are numerous legitimate extras for airport journeys, luggage etc.

By ferry

The simplest way to get to Athens from **Pireás** is by metro. Trains run from 6am to midnight. For the airport, take express bus #E96 (every 20min 7am–9pm, every 40min 9pm–7am). Taxis between Pireás and central Athens should cost around €8, including baggage: getting a taxi when a ferry arrives is no easy matter, though – you'll need to be pushy, and almost certainly have to share.

City transport

Athens is served by slow but wide-ranging **buses**, a curiously anachronistic but effective **trolley bus** network and a fast **metro** system which is currently undergoing massive expansion; **taxis** fill in the gaps. As well as the metro/rail link to the airport, there are two new **tram** lines: one following the line of Leofóros Syngroú from the centre to Fáliro on the coast near Pireás; the other running from Fáliro through the seaside suburbs to Glyfádha. Public transport networks operate from around 5am to midnight, with only the airport buses running in the small hours. You need to buy a **ticket** from a street kiosk or metro station before you travel.

A good website to start your planning is ⓦwww.oasa.gr/uk/index_gr.asp, an English version of the official Greek **Athens Urban Transport Organisation** website.

The metro

The Athens metro (ⓦwww.ametro.gr) has been much expanded in recent years, with the long-awaited addition of two completely new lines and a couple of new stops added to the original Line 1. The system is a huge success: designed to handle almost half a million passengers a day, it is fast, quiet and user-friendly. The stations are often attractions in their own right – displaying artefacts discovered in their excavation and other items of local interest.

Further extensions to lines 2 and 3 are underway, and likely to open in stages over the next few years. Meanwhile, **Line 1** (green) runs from Pireás in the south to Kifissiá in the north; useful stops in the centre include Thissío, Monastiráki,

Tickets and passes

Athens' public transport is good value, especially with judicious use of the various **passes** available. While most of the major sites are within walking distance of each other, the expansion of the metro means that it often makes more sense to jump on a train to go from, say, Omónia to Sýndagma, than sweating it out on the streets. If you can figure out the bus and trolley system, it's even cheaper to use them instead.

The easiest and, for most visitors, best-value ticket is the **24-hour *imerísio***. This costs €2.90 and can be used on all buses, trolleybuses and the metro, as well as for a single trip to the airport. You validate it once, on starting your first journey, and it is valid for 24 hours from then – cancel it again if you take the airport bus. The ticket can be bought from any metro ticket office and many places where bus tickets are sold (see below) – you can buy several at once and then cancel them as necessary. There's also a monthly pass for €35, or €17.50 for buses only.

Otherwise, individual **metro tickets** cost €0.60 on Line 1 for journeys within two of its three zones (this will get you from the centre to either end of the line), €0.70 for any other journey (valid for ninety minutes from validation, for travel in one direction – ie you can change lines, but you can't go somewhere and come back). They're available from machines and ticket offices in any metro station, and must be validated before you start your journey, in the machines at the top of the stairs.

Bus tickets cost €0.45 and must be bought in advance from kiosks, certain shops and newsagents, or from the limited number of booths run by bus personnel near major stops – look for the brown, red and white logo proclaiming *Isitíria edhó* (tickets here). They're sold individually or in bundles of ten, and must be cancelled in a special machine when boarding. Cancelled tickets apply only to a particular journey and vehicle; there are no transfers.

On both bus and metro, fare-dodgers risk an on-the-spot **fine** equivalent to forty times the current fare.

Omónia and Viktorías. **Line 2** (red) runs from Sepólia to Dháfni, with central stops at Omónia, Sýndagma and Akrópoli at the foot of the Acropolis. **Line 3** (blue) extends from Monastiráki northeast to Ethnikí Ámyna and to Dhoukíssis Plakentías, with trains continuing from there via new suburban rail lines to the **airport**.

Buses and trolleys

Athens' **bus network**, serving hundreds of routes from the centre out into the straggling suburbs and beyond, has also benefitted from much-needed investment over recent years and the city now boasts a fleet of modern, comfortable buses, including a growing number of "green" vehicles running off natural gas. There's also a substantial **trolley bus** network, long since disappeared from the streets of most cities in Europe. The original Russian-made trolley buses of yesteryear have almost all been replaced by modern and more comfortable air-conditioned versions. Using electricity as their primary source of power, they're also equipped with diesel engines to manoeuvre around traffic problems.

The bad news is that the system is pretty confusing – it's not always obvious which bus to take or where to catch it – and that buses can be very crowded at peak times (7–8.30am & 1.30–3pm), unbearably hot in summer traffic jams, and chronically plagued by strikes and slow-downs; walking is often a better option, particularly in the city centre.

Among the handiest of the trolley bus routes are the #1, which connects the Larísis train station with Omónia, Sýndagma and Koukáki; and #2–#5 and #12, which all link Sýndagma with Omónia and the National Archeological Museum on Patisíon. Where other buses are convenient, we've detailed them in the text, and most bus stops now show the routes of the main services using them. Check the "Going Places" section of Ⓦwww.oasa.gr/uk/index_gr.asp for details of all transport options to just about anywhere in Athens.

Taxis

Athenian **taxis** have a rather dodgy reputation – due more to the cavalier attitude of the drivers than to the cars themselves. Drivers are notoriously capricious and will often take you only where they want to go rather than to your exact destination – justifiable to a point in a city where getting from A to B can take up to a couple of hours, but not helpful for foreign visitors. Few drivers speak English, many still smoke in the cab despite an official ban, and an unscrupulous minority will rip you off mercilessly. Prior to the 2004 Olympics, all Athenian taxi drivers were supposed to have attended "charm school" for re-education, but few locals expected to notice much change.

That said, Athens' cabs are still among the cheapest of any European capital – **fares** around the city centre rarely run above €3, with a journey to the airport only €12–15 and Pireás €6–8 from the centre. The exact amount is determined by the pickup point and the amount of luggage, with a minimum fare of €1.50. All officially licensed cabs are yellow, with a special black-on-yellow number plate beginning with the letter "T" (some older red-on-white plates are also still in circulation). You can wave them down on the street, pick them up from ranks at the train stations, airport or the National Gardens on the corner of Sýndagma, or get your hotel to phone one for you (adding a €1.50 surcharge to the fare). They are most elusive during rush hours, or when it rains.

Make sure the **meter** is switched on when you get in, with its display visible and properly zeroed. There are no fixed-price rides in and around Athens – use of the meter is compulsory, so if it's "not working", find another taxi.

Attempts at overcharging tourists are particularly common with small-hours arrivals at the airport and Pireás. A threat to have hotel staff or the tourist police adjudicate usually elicits co-operation, as they will very likely take your side and the police have the power to revoke a driver's operating permit. In case of a dispute, make an obvious written note of the vehicle's number plate details.

Every taxi must have a dash-mounted plastic placard listing regular rates and **extra charges** in English and Greek. Legitimate surcharges can considerably bump up the final bill from the total shown on the meter. These include extra charges for journeys to or from the airport and train or ferry terminals, and for each piece of luggage over 10kg; the rate per kilometre almost doubles between midnight and 5am, and there are Easter and Christmas bonuses, which seem to extend for a week or two either side of the actual date.

To help make ends meet on government-regulated fare limits, taxi-drivers often pick up **extra passengers** along the way. There is no fare-sharing: each passenger or group of passengers pays the full fare for their journey. So if you're picked up by an already-occupied taxi, memorize the meter reading at once; you'll pay from that point on, plus the €0.80 minimum. When hailing an occupied taxi, shout out your destination so the driver can decide whether he wants your custom or not.

Information

The **Greek National Tourist Office** (GNTO; Ellinikós Organismós Tourismoú or EOT in Greek; Ⓦwww.gnto.gr) has a brand new central information office at Amalías 26, just off Sýndagma (Ⓣ210 33 10 392). This is a useful first stop for information, and they have a good free map as well as information sheets on current opening hours, bus and ferry schedules, and so on. There's also Internet access. If you are arriving by plane, you could also call in at the airport branch (see p.165).

Useful **maps** to complement those in this guide include the *Rough Guide City Map* of Athens (Ⓦwww.roughguides.com) – full-colour, non-tearable, weatherproof and pocket-sized, detailing attractions, places to shop, eat, drink and sleep, as well as the city streets – or the city maps produced by Emvelia (Ⓦwww.emvelia.gr) or Falkplan. These and others should be available from good local bookshops and some kiosks: the best source is the top floor of the Eleftheroudakis bookshop at Panepistimíou 17, between Sýndagma and Omónia.

Useful sources of information for **what's on** include the English-language daily *Athens News*, whose Friday edition has a complete events programme for the weekend. Much more extensive listings, but in Greek only, can be found in *Athinorama* or *Time Out Athens*, both of which have screening times for all films and exhaustive catalogues of nightspots, restaurant, music and events. They're published weekly on Thursdays.

Directory

AIRLINES Aegean, Vouliagménis 572 Ⓣ210 99 88 300, reservations Ⓣ801 11 20 000, airport Ⓣ210 35 30 101; British Airways, Themistokléous 1, Glyfádha Ⓣ210 89 06 666, airport Ⓣ210 32 30 453; Delta, Óthonos 4 Ⓣ210 33 11 668, reservations Ⓣ800 44 129 506; EasyJet, airport only Ⓣ210 35 30 300; Hellas Jet, Michalakópoulou 91, Ilísia Ⓣ210 74 57 700, reservations Ⓣ801 11 53 000, airport Ⓣ210 35 30 815-9; Olympic, Fillelínon 15 Ⓣ210 92

67 663, reservations ☎210 96 66 666, airport 210 93 68 424; Singapore Airlines, Xenofóndos 9 ☎210 37 28 000; Thai, Venizélou 32, Glyfádha ☎210 96 92 010.

AIRPORT ENQUIRIES ☎210 35 31 000 for airline offices at the airport, ☎210 35 30 000 for flight schedules.

AMERICAN EXPRESS Poste restante and money changing at the main branch at Ermoú 2 (1st floor), on the corner of Sýndagma Square. Two offices at the airport are open 24hr.

BANKS AND EXCHANGE Most banks have 24hr ATMs that accept debit cards. Banking hours are typically Mon–Thurs 8.30am–2.30pm and Fri 8.30am–2pm. Exchange bureaux are open during regular business hours throughout the city and are far quicker than banks – but check the commission and exchange rate. Most hotels will also exchange currency, though usually at a poor rate, and getting cash on a credit card is very expensive.

BEACHES Almost all the good beaches in and around Athens demand payment for entry, for which you'll get a clean beach, a lounger, somewhere to buy food and drink, and facilities including beach volleyball and all sorts of watersports. Some of the fanciest charge €10 per person at weekends; more basic places charge €3–5. There are plenty of spots to swim for free, but this may mean from the rocks, or involve a long hike from the road. On summer weekends, every beach – and the roads to them – will be packed.

CAR RENTAL Most car rental companies have offices near the top of Leofóros Syngroú, including Antena at no.52 (☎210 92 32 544); Budget (no.8, ☎210 92 14 771); EuropCar (no.43, ☎210 95 88 990; Hertz (no.12, ☎210 92 20 102); Holiday Autos (no.8, ☎210 22 23 088); Thrifty (no.25, ☎210 92 46 001); Sixt (no.23, ☎210 92 20 121); and Status (no.40, ☎210 92 24 345).

CINEMA Athens has dozens of indoor cinemas, and in summer many outdoor screens showing second-run offerings, classics and cult films, while festivals feature prominent European and American directors. Films are always shown in the original language with Greek subtitles, and admission is €6–8. Downtown indoor cinemas are concentrated on the three main thoroughfares connecting Omónia and Sýndagma; and in Ambelókipi, around the junctions of Leofóros Alexándhras and Kifissías. Central and reliable outdoor venues include Cine Paris, on the roof at Kydathinéon 22, Pláka; Apostólou Pávlou 7, Thissío; Panathinea, Mavromiháli 165, Neápoli; Zefyros, Tróön 36, Thissío (good for film noir and Fifties oldies); Vox on the platía and Riviera at Valtetsíou 46, both in Exárhia.

CLASSICAL MUSIC The summer-long Hellenic Festival hosts many of Athens' finest classical performances, and the city's concert hall – the Mégaro Mousikís on Vassilísis Sofías in Ilísia by the metro station that bears its name – also has a full season running throughout the winter months.

DANCE The one outstanding dance event worth catching is the Dora Stratou Ethnic Dance Company performing in their own theatre at Arakínthou and Voutié on Filopáppou Hill (☎210 92 14 650). Performances (late May to late Sept Tues–Sat 9.30pm, Sun 8.15pm; €13) combine traditional music, fine choreography and gorgeous costumes. To reach the theatre, walk along the south flank of the Acropolis until you see the signs. Tickets can almost always be picked up at the door.

DISABLED TRAVELLERS Hotels throughout Athens were refurbished in the run-up to the Olympics, and many have accessible rooms and other facilities. However, the infrastructure of the city is tricky for people in wheelchairs or with limited mobility. Pavements are rarely smooth, there are many steep streets, and the ground at most archeological sites is extremely uneven. The new metro has excellent lifts from pavement level direct to the platforms, but often a large gap between the platform and the train.

EMBASSIES & CONSULATES Australia, Dhimitríou Soútsou 37 ☎210 64 50 405; Canada, Ioánnou Yennadhíou 4 ☎210 72

73 400; Ireland, Vasiléos Konstandínou 7 ☎210 72 32 771; New Zealand (consulate), Xenías 24, Ambelókipi ☎210 77 10 112; UK, Ploútarhou 1, Kolonáki ☎210 72 72 600; US, Vasilíssis Sofías 91 ☎210 72 12 951.

EMERGENCIES Ambulance ☎166; Fire ☎199; Police ☎100; Tourist police ☎171.

FERRIES Almost any travel agent in Athens can sell you a ferry ticket, but they don't necessarily represent all companies, so be sure you're not taking a roundabout route. In Pireás, there's far more choice: unless you want a cabin, there's rarely any need to book ahead.

FESTIVALS The great event of the Greek cultural year is the Hellenic Festival, which runs from June to September every year. It encompasses a broad spectrum of cultural events, most famously ancient Greek theatre (performed, in modern Greek, at the Herodes Atticus Theatre on the south slope of the Acropolis), but also traditional and contemporary dance, classical music, jazz, traditional Greek music and even rock. Other festival venues include the open-air Lykavitós Theatre on Lykavitós Hill, the mansion of the Duchess of Plaisance in Pendéli and the ancient theatre at Epidauros (see p.144). Programmes of performances and tickets are best picked up as soon as you arrive in the city, or even booked before you arrive. The festival box office is in the arcade at 39 Panepistimíou (Mon–Fri 8.30am–4pm, Sat 9am–2.30pm; ☎210 32 21 459, Ⓦwww.hellenicfestival.gr). You can also buy tickets at the Herodes Atticus box office (daily 9am–2pm & 6–9pm; ☎210 32 32 771) or at Epidauros.

FOOTBALL The three major Athens teams – Panathinaïkós, AEK and Olympiakós – dominate Greek football. Panathinaïkós are the most central, at Leofóros Alexándhras in Ambelókipi (right beside the metro station). AEK play at the Níkos Goumás stadium in Néa Filadhélfia (metro to Perissós station, from where it's less than ten minutes' walk). Olympiakós' home is the Karaïskáki stadium in Néo Fáliro (right opposite the metro), newly refurbished for the Olympics.

INTERNET There are plenty of Internet Cafés throughout central Athens, mostly charging around €2–4 per hour. They generally have fast connections and modern machines, but are often smoky. Some of the more central and reliable are: Easy Internet Café, west side of Platía Sýndagma above Everest; Internet World, Pandhróssou 29, Pláka; QuickNet, Gladstónos 4, Omónia; Sky Net, Voulís 30, Sýndagma; C@fé 4U, Ippokrátous 44, Exarhía; British Council, Platía Kolonáki (free access during library hours, Mon–Fri 10am–7pm, Sat 10.30am–2pm).

MAIL Post office hours are typically Mon–Fri 7.30am–2pm; some main branches open evenings and Sat mornings. The busy main office on Sýndagma Square has long queues – it's worth heading to the quieter branch nearby at Níkis 37. Overseas rates start at €0.65 for a postcard sent anywhere in the world – you can usually buy a stamp (*grammatósimo*) from the vendor of the card.

MARKETS Many Athenian neighbourhoods have a weekly *laïkí agorá* – **street market** – usually running from 7am to 2pm. The most centrally located (listed by street name and area) are: Hánsen in Patissíon (Mon); Lésvou in Kypséli and Láskou in Pangráti (both Tues); Xenokrátous in Kolonáki, Dragoúmi in Ilísia, Tsámi Karatássou in Koukáki and Arhimídhous in Mets (all Fri); and Plakendías in Ambelókipi (one of the largest) and Kallidhromíou in Exárhia, both on Saturday.

MONEY Standard currency in Greece is the euro, divided into 100 *leptá* (cents). You may still see prices quoted in dhrachmas (the old currency) and many till receipts continue to show the value in both, but the old notes and coins are no longer valid. The major credit cards are accepted virtually everywhere, though perhaps with reluctance at the cheaper tavernas and bars.

OPENING HOURS Traditionally shops and offices open from 8.30 or 9am until 1.30 or 2.30pm, when there is a long break for the hottest part of the day. Most places, except banks and government offices, then reopen in the late afternoon, from about 5.30 to 8.30pm; they're closed on Sundays, and often on Saturday, Monday and Wednesday afternoons. However, increasing numbers of places, especially in the city centre and above all the tourist shops in Pláka, now remain open throughout the day. Hours can also vary between summer and winter (usually Oct–March & April–Sept).

PHARMACIES The Marinópoulos branches on Patisíon and Panepistimíou are particularly good and also sell homeopathic remedies. Bakákos, on Platía Omonías is the largest general pharmacy in Athens and stocks just about everything. All pharmacies display a daily list of those open after-hours.

PUBLIC HOLIDAYS Official holidays are: January 1; January 6; March 25; the first Monday of Lent (variable Feb/March); Easter weekend (variable March/April); May 1; Pentecost or Whit Monday (fifty days after Easter); August 15; October 28; December 25 and 26. Many Athenians take their holidays at Easter and during August, when some shops and restaurants will be closed.

SKIING A day-trip to ski from Athens is easily arranged in winter: the main centre at Mount Parnassós (p.143) is accessible either by car or on an organized tour. To avoid the hordes, go during the week.

SMOKING Greeks smoke heavily, often in crowded public places such as cafés, restaurants and bars. Public transport is non-smoking, as are many offices, but only a small minority of places to eat or drink will have effective non-smoking areas.

TELEPHONES Phonecards (*tilekárta*) for public phones are available from kiosks and small shops, starting at €3. For international calls, though, an international calling card (such as AT&T) is usually better value: if you already have one, you'll need to know the access code for Greece. For the domestic operator, call ☎132; for the international operator, call ☎139. Mobile phones are ubiquitous in Athens, and if you have an international roaming facility, you should have no problem using yours while here.

THEATRE The contemporary Greek theatre scene is unlikely to be accessible unless your Greek is fluent. As with Greek music, it is essentially a winter pursuit; in summer, the only productions tend to be satirical and (to outsiders) totally incomprehensible revues. However, well worth catching is the Classical drama staged (June–Aug Fri & Sat nights) at the spectacular ancient theatre in Epidauros (see p.144). For big productions you're best getting your tickets in advance as seats can sell out quickly.

TIME Greek summer time begins at 2am on the last Sunday in March, when the clocks go forward one hour, and ends at 2am the last Sunday in October when they go back. Greek time is thus always two hours ahead of Britain. For North America, the difference is seven hours for Eastern Standard Time, ten hours for Pacific Standard Time, with an extra hour plus or minus for those few weeks in April when one place is on daylight saving and the other isn't.

TOURS Most travel agencies offer a variety of tours out of Athens, as well as day- or half-day tours of the city. The latter normally include a bus drive around the highlights and a guided tour of the Acropolis and its museum for around €30. You could also take the "Happy Train" ride, which sets out from the Platía Paliás Agorás (on Eólou, just off Adhrianoú) and clatters past most of the major sites for an hour or so (€5, children €3).

Language

Language

Basics

You can get by in Athens speaking only English – in the tourist areas certainly there'll always be someone who can speak it fluently. Away from the centre you may struggle occasionally, but even here an English-speaker is rarely far away. However, the effort of mastering a few Greek words is well repaid, and will transform your status from that of dumb turístas to the more honourable one of xénos/xéni, a word which can mean foreigner, traveller and guest all rolled into one.

The Rough Guide *Greek Dictionary Phrasebook* is full of more phrases that you'll need. It also fills you in on cultural know-how and is sensibly transliterated.

Pronunciation

On top of the usual difficulties of learning a new language, Greek presents the additional problem of an entirely separate **alphabet**. Despite initial appearances, this is in practice fairly easily mastered and is a skill that will help enormously if you are going to get around independently. In addition, certain combinations of letters have unexpected results. Remember that the correct **stress** (marked with an accent) is crucial. With the right sounds but the wrong stress people will either fail to understand you, or else understand something quite different from what you intended – there are numerous pairs of words with the same spelling and phonemes, distinguished only by their stress.

Set out below is the Greek alphabet, the system of transliteration used in this book, and a brief aid to pronunciation.

Greek	Transliteration	Pronounced
Α, α	a	a as in father
Β, β	v	v as in vet
Γ, γ	y/g	y as in yes except before consonants or a, o or ou when it's a breathy g, approximately as in gap
Δ, δ	dh	th as in then
Ε, ε	e	e as in get
Ζ, ζ	z	z sound
Η, η	i	i as in ski
Θ, θ	th	th as in theme
Ι, ι	i	i as in ski
Κ, κ	k	k sound
Λ, λ	l	l sound
Μ, μ	m	m sound
Ν, ν	n	n sound
Ξ, ξ	x	x sound
Ο, ο	o	o as in toad

Π, π	p	p sound
Ρ, ρ	r	r sound
Σ, σ, ς	s	s sound, except z before m or g; single sigma has the same phonic value as double sigma
Τ, τ	t	t sound
Υ, υ	y	y as in barely
Φ, φ	f	f sound
Χ, χ	h before vowels, kh before consonants	harsh h sound, like ch in loch
Ψ, ψ	ps	ps as in lips
Ω, ω	o	o as in toad, indistinguishable from ο

Combinations and diphthongs

ΑΙ, αι	e	e as in hey
ΑΥ, αυ	av/af	av or af depending on following consonant
ΕΙ, ει	i	long i, exactly ι or η
ΕΥ, ευ	ev/ef	ev or ef, depending on following consonant
ΟΙ, οι	i	long i, exactly like ι or η
ΟΥ, ου	ou	ou as in tourist
ΓΓ, γγ	ng	ng as in angle; always medial
ΓΚ, γκ	g/ng	g as in goat at the beginning of a word, ng in the middle
ΜΠ, μπ	b/mb	b at the beginning of a word, mb in the middle
ΝΤ, ντ	d/nd	d at the beginning of a word, nd in the middle
ΤΣ, τσ	ts	ts as in hits
ΤΖ, τζ	tz	dg as in judge, j as in jam in some dialects

Words and phrases

Basics

Yes	Né
Certainly	Málista
No	Óhi
Please	Parakaló
OK, agreed	Endáxi
Thank you (very much)	Efharistó (polý)
I (don't) understand	(Dhén) Katalavéno
Excuse me	Parakaló, mípos
Do you speak English?	Miláte angliká?
Sorry, excuse me	Signómi
Today	Símera
Tomorrow	Ávrio
Yesterday	Khthés
Now	Tóra
Later	Argótera
Open	Anikhtó
Closed	Klistó
Day	Méra
Night	Níkhta
In the morning	Tó proï
In the afternoon	Tó apóyevma
In the evening	Tó vrádhi
Here	Edhó
There	Ekí
This one	Aftó
That one	Ekíno
Good	Kaló
Bad	Kakó
Big	Megálo
Small	Mikró
More	Perisótero
Less	Ligótero
A little	Lígo
A lot	Polý
Cheap	Ftinó
Expensive	Akrivó
Hot	Zestó

Cold	Krýo	**Pharmacy**	Farmakío
With (together)	Mazí (mé)	**Post office**	Tahydhromío
Without	Horís	**Stamps**	Gramatósima
Quickly	Grígora	**Petrol station**	Venzinádhiko
Slowly	Sigá	**Bank**	Trápeza
Mr/Mrs	Kýrios/Kyría	**Money**	Leftá/khrímata
Miss	Dhespinís	**Toilet**	Toualéta
To eat/drink	Trógo/píno	**Police**	Astynomía
Bakery	Foúrnos, psomádhiko	**Doctor**	Yiatrós
		Hospital	Nosokomío

Requests

To ask a question, it's simplest to start with *parakaló*, then name the thing you want in an interrogative tone.

Where is the bakery?	Parakaló, o foúrnos?	**How much?**	Póso?
Can you show me the road to . . . ?	Parakaló, ó dhrómos yiá . . . ?	**When?**	Póte?
We'd like a room for two	Parakaló, éna dhomátio yiá dhýo átoma	**Why?**	Yiatí?
May I have a kilo of oranges?	Parakaló, éna kiló portokália?	**At what time . . . ?**	Tí óra . . . ?
Where?	Poú?	**What is/ Which is . . . ?**	Tí íne/Pió íne . . . ?
How?	Pós?	**How much does it cost?**	Póso káni?
How many?	Póssi, pósses or póssa?	**What time does it open?**	Tí óra aníyi?
		What time does it close?	Tí óra klíni?

Conversation

By far the most common greeting, on meeting and parting, is *yiá sou/yiá sas* – literally "health to you". Incidentally, the approaching party utters the first greeting, not those seated at sidewalk *kafenío* tables or doorsteps.

Hello	Hérete	**Speak slower, please**	Parakaló, miláte pió sigá
Good morning	Kalí méra	**How do you say it in Greek?**	Pós léyete stá Elliniká?
Good evening	Kalí spéra	**I don't know**	Dhén xéro
Good night	Kalí níkhta	**See you tomorrow**	Thá sé dhó ávrio
Goodbye	Adío	**See you soon**	Kalí andhámosi
How are you?	Tí kánis/Tí kánete?	**Let's go**	Páme
I'm fine	Kalá íme	**Please help me**	Parakaló, ná mé voithíste
And you?	Ké essís?		
What's your name?	Pós se léne?		
My name is . . .	Mé léne . . .		

Greek's Greek

There are numerous words and phrases which you will hear constantly, even if you rarely have the chance to use them. These are a few of the most common.

Éla!	Come (literally) but also "Speak to me!", "You don't say!", and so on.
Oríste!	Literally, "Indicate!"; in effect, "What can I do for you?"
Embrós! or Léyete!	Standard phone responses.
Tí néa?	What's new?
Tí yínete?	What's going on (here)?
Étsi k'étsi	So-so.
Ópa!	Whoops! Watch it!
Po-po-po!	Expression of dismay or concern, like French "O là là!".
Pedhí moú	My boy/girl, sonny, friend etc.
Maláka(s)	Literally "wanker", but often used (don't try it!) as an informal term of address.
Sigá sigá	Take your time, slow down.
Kaló taxídhi	Bon voyage.

Accommodation

Hotel	Xenodhohío
Inn	Xenón(as)
Youth hostel	Xenónas neótitos
A room . . .	Éna dhomátio . . .
for one/two/ three people	yiá éna/dhýo/tría átoma
for one/two/ three nights	yiá mía/dhýo/trís vradhiés
with a double	mé megálo kreváti
with a shower	mé doús
Hot water	Zestó neró
Cold water	Krýo neró
Air conditioning	Klimatismós
Fan	Anamistíra
Can I see it?	Boró ná tó dhó?
Can we camp here?	Boroúme na váloume ti skiní edhó?
Campsite	Kámping/Kataskínosi
Tent	Skiní

Travel

Aeroplane	Aeropláno
Bus, coach	Leoforío, púlman
Car	Aftokínito, amáxi
Motorbike, scooter	Mihanáki, papáki
Taxi	Taxí
Ship	Plío/vapóri/karávi
High-speed catamaran	Tahýplio
Hydrofoil	Dhelfíni
Train	Tréno
Train station	Sidhirodhromikós stathmós
Bicycle	Podhílato
Hitching	Otostóp
On foot	Mé tá pódhia
Trail	Monopáti
Bus station	Praktorío leoforíon, KTEL
Bus stop	Stássi
Harbour	Limáni
What time does it leave?	Ti óra févyi?
What time does it arrive?	Ti óra ftháni?
How many kilometres?	Póssa hiliómetra?
How many hours?	Pósses óres?
Where are you going?	Poú pás?
I'm going to . . .	Páo stó . . .
I want to get off at . . .	Thélo ná katévo stó . . .
The road to . . .	O dhrómos yiá . . .
Near	Kondá
Far	Makriá
Left	Aristerá
Right	Dhexiá
Straight ahead	Katefthía, ísia
A ticket to . . .	Éna isitírio yiá . . .
A return ticket	Éna isitírio mé epistrofí
Beach	Paralía
Cave	Spiliá
Centre (of town)	Kéndro
Church	Eklissía
Sea	Thálassa
Village	Horió

Numbers

1	énas/éna/mía	30	triánda
2	dhýo	40	saránda
3	trís/tría	50	penínda
4	tésseres/téssera	60	exínda
5	pénde	70	evdhomínda
6	éxi	80	ogdhónda
7	eftá	90	enenínda
8	okhtó	100	ekató
9	ennéa (or more slangy, enyá)	150	ekatón penínda
10	dhéka	200	dhiakóssies/dhiakóssia
11	éndheka	500	pendakóssies/pendakóssia
12	dhódheka	1000	hílies/hília
13	dhekatrís	2000	dhýo hiliádhes
14	dhekatésseres	1,000,000	éna ekatomírio
20	íkossi	first	próto
21	íkossi éna (all compounds written separately thus)	second	dhéftero
		third	tríto

Days of the week and the time

Sunday	Kyriakí	**Twenty minutes to four**	Tésseres pará íkossi
Monday	Dheftéra	**Five minutes past seven**	Eftá ké pénde
Tuesday	Tríti	**Half past eleven**	Éndheka ké misí
Wednesday	Tetárti	**In half an hour**	Sé misí óra
Thursday	Pémpti	**In a quarter-hour**	S'éna tétarto
Friday	Paraskeví	**In two hours**	Sé dhýo óres
Saturday	Sávato		
What time is it?	Tí óra íne?		
One/two/three o'clock	Mía íy óra/dhýo iy óra/trís íy óra		

Months and seasons

Note that you may see hybrid forms of the months written on schedules or street signs; the below are the spoken demotic forms.

January	Yennáris	**September**	Septémvris
February	Fleváris	**October**	Októvrios
March	Mártis	**November**	Noémvris
April	Aprílis	**December**	Dhekémvris
May	Maïos	**Summer schedule**	Therinó dhromolóyio
June	Ioúnios	**Winter schedule**	Himerinó dhromolóyio
July	Ioúlios		
August	Ávgoustos		

Menu reader

Basics

Aláti	Salt	**Neró**	Water
Avgá	Eggs	**Psári(a)**	Fish
(Horís) ládhi	(Without) Oil	**Psomí**	Bread
Hortofágos	Vegetarian	**Olikís**	Wholemeal bread
Katálogo, lísta	Menu	**Sikalísio**	Rye bread
Kréas	Meat	**Thalassiná**	Seafood
Lahaniká	Vegetables	**Tyrí**	Cheese
O logariasmós	The bill	**Yiaoúrti**	Yogurt
Méli	Honey	**Záhari**	Sugar

Cooking terms

Akhnistó	Steamed	**Sti soúvla**	Spit-roasted
Makaronádha	Any pasta-based dish	**Stó foúrno**	Baked
Pastó	Marinated in salt	**Tiganitó**	Pan-fried
Psitó	Roasted	**Tís óras**	Grilled/fried to order
Saganáki	Cheese-based red sauce; or any fried cheese	**Yakhní**	Stewed in oil and tomato sauce
Skáras	Grilled	**Yemistá**	Stuffed (squid, vegetables, and so on)

Soups and starters

Avgolémono	Egg and lemon soup	**Mavromátika**	Black-eyed peas
Dolmádhes	Stuffed vine leaves	**Melitzanosaláta**	Aubergine/eggplant dip
Fasoládha	Bean soup	**Revytho-keftédhes**	Chickpea (garbanzo) patties
Fáva	Purée of yellow peas, served with onion and lemon	**Skordhaliá**	Garlic dip
Florínes	Canned red sweet Macedonian peppers	**Soúpa**	Soup
Hortópita	Turnover or pie stuffed with wild greens	**Taramosaláta**	Cod roe paté
Kafterí	Cheese dip with chili added	**Trahanádhes**	Crushed wheat and milk soup, sweet or savoury
Kápari	Pickled caper leaves	**Tyrokafterí**	Cheese dip with chilli, different from *kopanistí*
Kopanistí, khtypití	Pungent, fermented cheese purée	**Tzatzíki**	Yogurt and cucumber dip
Krítamo	Rock samphire	**Tzirosaláta**	cured mackerel dip

Vegetables

Anginámes	Artichokes	**Domátes**	Tomatoes
Angoúri	Cucumber	**Fakés**	Lentils
Ánitho	Dill	**Fasolákia**	French (green) beans
Bámies	Okra, ladies' fingers	**Horiátiki (saláta)**	Greek salad (with olives, feta etc)
Bouréki, bourekákia	Courgette/zucchini, potato and cheese pie	**Hórta**	Greens (usually wild), steamed
Briám	Ratatouille		

Kolokythákia	Courgette/zucchini
Koukiá	Broad beans
Maroúli	Lettuce
Melitzánes imám	Aubergine/eggplant slices baked with onion, garlic and copious olive oil
Patátes	Potatoes
Piperiés	Peppers
Pligoúri, pinigoúri	Bulgur wheat
Radhíkia	Wild chicory – a common *hórta*
Rýzi, piláfi	Rice (usually with *sáltsa* – sauce)
Rókka	Rocket
Saláta	Salad
Spanáki	Spinach
Vlíta	Notchweed – another common *hórta*
Yígandes	White haricot beans

Fish and seafood

Astakós	Aegean lobster
Atherína	Sand smelt
Bakaliáros	Cod or hake, usually latter
Barbóuni	Red mullet
Fangrí	Common bream
Foúskes	*Uovo de mare* (Italian), *violet* (French); no English equivalent for this invertebrate.
Galéos	Dogfish, hound shark, tope
Garídhes	Shrimp, prawns
Gávros	Mild anchovy
Glóssa	Sole
Gónos, gonákia	Any hatchling fish
Gópa	Bogue
Kalamarákia	Baby squid
Kalamária	Squid
Karavídhes	Crayfish
Kefalás	Axillary bream
Koliós	Chub mackerel
Koutsomoúra	Goatfish (small red mullet)
Kydhónia	Cockles
Lakérdha	Light-fleshed bonito, marinated
Marídhes	Picarel
Melanoúri	Saddled bream
Ménoula	Sprat
Mýdhia	Mussels
Okhtapódhi	Octopus
Pandelís	Corvina; also called sykiós
Platý	Skate, ray
Sardhélles	Sardines
Sargós	White bream
Seláhi	Skate, ray
Skáros	Parrotfish
Skathári	Black bream
Skoumbrí	Atlantic mackerel
Soupiá	Cuttlefish
Spiníalo, spinóalo	Marinated *foúskes*
Synagrídha	Dentex
Tsipoúra	Gilt-head bream
Vátos	Skate, ray
Xifías	Swordfish
Yermanós	Leatherback

Meat dishes

Arní	Lamb
Bekrí mezé	Pork chunks in red sauce
Biftéki	Hamburger
Brizóla	Pork or beef chop
Hirinó	Pork
Keftédhes	Meatballs
Kokorétsi	Liver/offal roulade, spit-roasted
Kopsídha	Lamb shoulder chops
Kotópoulo	Chicken
Kounélli	Rabbit
Loukánika	Spicy course-ground sausages
Moskhári	Veal
Moussakás	Aubergine, potato and lamb-mince casserole with bechamel topping
Païdhákia	Rib chops, lamb or goat
Papoutsákia	Stuffed aubergine/eggplant "shoes" – like *moussakás* without bechamel
Pastítsio	Macaroni pie baked with minced meat
Pastourmás	Cured, highly spiced meat; traditionally camel, nowadays beef
Patsás	Tripe and trotter soup

Psaronéfri	Pork tenderloin medallions
Salingária	Garden snails
Soutzoukákia	Minced meat rissoles/beef patties
Spetzofáï	Sausage and pepper stew
Stifádho	Meat stew with tomato and onions
Sykóti	Liver
Tiganiá	Meat chunks, usually pork, fried in its own fat
Tziyéro sarmás	Lamb's liver in cabbage
Youvétsi	Baked clay casserole of meat and *kritharáki* (short pasta)

Sweets and desserts

Baklavás	Honey and nut pastry
Bougátsa	Salt or sweet cream pie served warm with sugar and cinammon
Galaktobóureko	Custard pie
Halvás	Sweetmeat of sesame or semolina
Karydhópita	Walnut cake
Kréma	Custard
Loukoumádhes	Dough fritters in honey syrup and sesame seeds
Pagotó	Ice cream
Pastélli	Sesame and honey bar
Ravaní	Spongecake, lightly syruped
Ryzógalo	Rice pudding

Fruit and nuts

Akhládhia	Big pears
Aktinídha	Kiwis
Fistíkia	Pistachio nuts
Fráoules	Strawberries
Karpoúzi	Watermelon
Kerásia	Cherries
Krystália	Miniature pears
Kydhóni	Quince
Lemónia	Lemons
Míla	Apples
Pepóni	Melon
Portokália	Oranges
Rodhákino	Peach
Sýka	Figs
Stafýlia	Grapes

Cheese

Ayeladhinó	Cow's-milk cheese
Féta	Salty, white cheese
Graviéra	Gruyère-type hard cheese
Katsikísio	Goat cheese
Kasséri	Medium-sharp cheese
Myzíthra	Sweet cream cheese
Próvio	Sheep's cheese

Drinks

Alisfakiá	Island sage tea
Boukáli	Bottle
Býra	Beer
Gála	Milk
Frappé	Iced coffee
Galakakáo	Chocolate milk
Gazóza	Generic fizzy drink
Kafés	Coffee
Krasí	Wine
áspro	white
kokkinélli/rozé	rosé
kókkino/mávro	red
Limonádha	Lemonade
Metalikó neró	Mineral water
Portokaládha	Orangeade
Potíri	Glass
Stinyássas!	Cheers!
Tsáï	Tea
Tsáï vounoú	"Mountain" (mainland sage) tea

Index and small print

A Rough Guide to Rough Guides

Athens DIRECTIONS is published by Rough Guides. The first *Rough Guide to Greece*, published in 1982, was a student scheme that became a publishing phenomenon. The immediate success of the book – with numerous reprints and a Thomas Cook prize shortlisting – spawned a series that rapidly covered dozens of destinations. Rough Guides had a ready market among low-budget backpackers, but soon also acquired a much broader and older readership that relished Rough Guides' wit and inquisitiveness as much as their enthusiastic, critical approach. Everyone wants value for money, but not at any price. Rough Guides soon began supplementing the "rougher" information about hostels and low-budget listings with the kind of detail on restaurants and quality hotels that independent-minded visitors on any budget might expect, whether on business in New York or trekking in Thailand. These days the guides offer recommendations from shoestring to luxury and a large number of destinations around the globe, including almost every country in the Americas and Europe, more than half of Africa and most of Asia and Australasia. Rough Guides now publish:

- Travel guides to more than 200 worldwide destinations
- Dictionary phrasebooks to 22 major languages
- Maps printed on rip-proof and waterproof Polyart™ paper
- Music guides running the gamut from Opera to Elvis
- Reference books on topics as diverse as the Weather and Shakespeare
- World Music CDs in association with World Music Network

Visit **www.roughguides.com** to see our latest publications.

Publishing Information

This 1st edition published May 2004 by **Rough Guides Ltd**, 80 Strand, London WC2R 0RL.
345 Hudson St, 4th Floor, New York, NY 10014, USA.

Distributed by the Penguin Group
Penguin Books Ltd, 80 Strand, London WC2R 0RL
Penguin Group (USA), 375 Hudson Street, NY 10014, USA
Penguin Group (Australia), 487 Maroondah Highway, PO Box 257, Ringwood, Victoria 3134, Australia
Penguin Group (Canada), 10 Alcorn Avenue, Toronto, Ontario, Canada M4V 1E4
Penguin Group (NZ), 182–190 Wairau Road, Auckland 10, New Zealand
Typeset in Bembo and Helvetica to an original design by Henry Iles.
Printed and bound in Italy by Graphicom

192pp includes index
A catalogue record for this book is available from the British Library

ISBN 1-84353-314-6

1 3 5 7 9 8 6 4 2

Help us update

We've gone to a lot of effort to ensure that the first edition of **Athens DIRECTIONS** is accurate and up-to-date. However, things change – places get "discovered", opening hours are notoriously fickle, restaurants and rooms raise prices or lower standards. If you feel we've got it wrong or left something out, we'd like to know, and if you can remember the address, the price, the time, the phone number, so much the better.

We'll credit all contributions, and send a copy of the next edition (or any other DIRECTIONS guide or Rough Guide if you prefer) for the best letters. Everyone who writes to us and isn't already a subscriber will receive a copy of our full-colour thrice-yearly newsletter. Please mark letters: "**Athens DIRECTIONS Update**" and send to: Rough Guides, 80 Strand, London WC2R 0RL, or Rough Guides, 4th Floor, 345 Hudson St, New York, NY 10014. Or send an email to **mail@roughguides.com**

Have your questions answered and tell others about your trip at **www.roughguides.atinfopop.com**

Rough Guide Credits

Text editors: Fran Sandham
Layout: Diana Jarvis, Daniel May
Photography: Paul Hellander
Cartography: Draughtsman Ltd, Miles Irving, Katie Lloyd-Jones, Ed Wright
Picture research: Jj Luck, Mark Thomas, Sharon Martins
Proofreader: Jan Wiltshire
Production: John McKay
Design: Henry Iles

The authors

John Fisher co-authored the first edition of the Rough Guide to Greece and has been inextricably linked with Rough Guides ever since. He lives in South London with his wife and two young sons.

Paul Hellander has been in and out of Greece for over thirty years, having graduated with a degree in Greek from Birmingham University. Imbued with an indelible love of Hellenism, Paul has a particular predilection for rocky islands, soaring mountains and the sleepless Olympic city of Athens.

Acknowledgements

From John: Thanks are due to more people than can be listed here, but above all to Dimitris Koutoulas, Calli Travlos and the staff of the GNTO in London, Nick Edwards, Kate Donnelly, Yiannis Mikhas and all at the prefecture of Pireás, Leonidas Tsagaris, Lena Zolota; to everyone at Rough Guides, especially Fran, Kate, Geoff, Ruth, Jj, Mark, Katie, Miles, Diana and Dan; and as always to A and the two Js for putting up with it for far too long.

From Paul: Many thanks to Angeliki Kanelli and Vana Kapsaski for sharing their Zografou home with me, as well as Marc Dubin and John Fisher for support and valuable insight.

Photo credits

Index

A

B

C

D

N

O

P

R

S

T

V

W

Z

DIRECTIONS on Screen

Put the guide on your computer or PDA

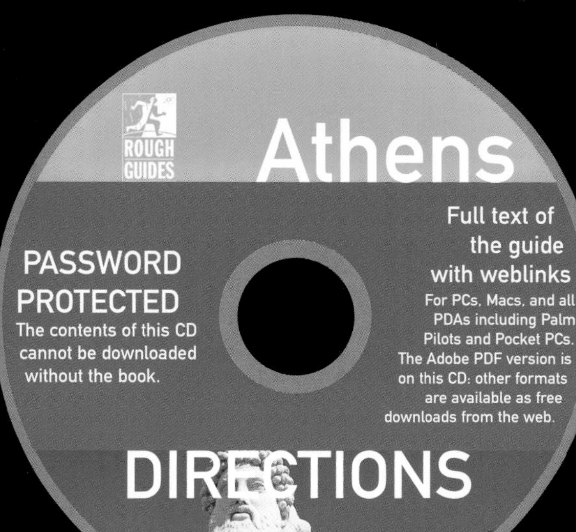

This CD contains the complete

Athens DIRECTIONS

formatted as Adobe pdf files, complete with maps and illustrations, and readable on any Windows or Mac-OS laptop or desktop computer. It also contains simple instructions for free downloads formatted for the Pocket PC and Palm platforms.

Insert the CD into any tray-operating CD-Rom drive. Full instructions supplied. Note on platforms: Adobe supports maps and illustrations and is compatible with both Macintosh and PC operating systems. Pocket PC, and Palm platforms support text only.